FANTASTIC ARCHITECTURE

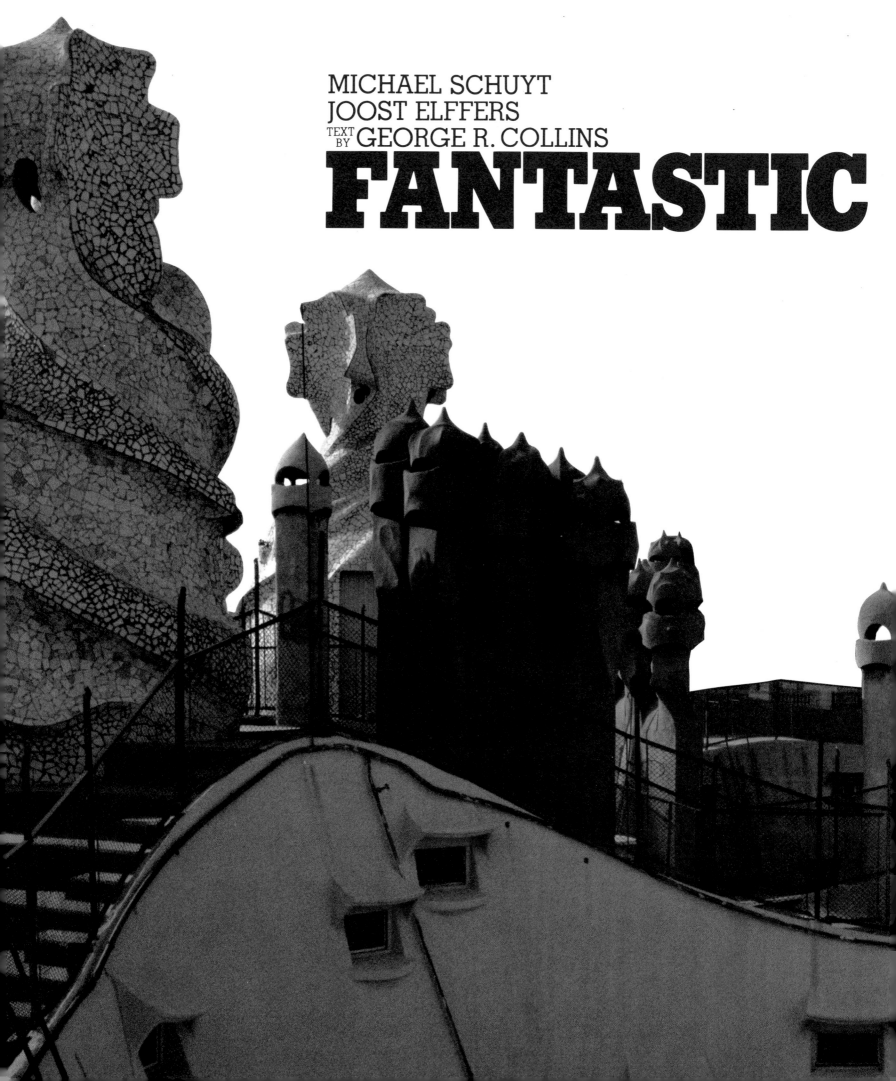

MICHAEL SCHUYT
JOOST ELFFERS
TEXT BY GEORGE R. COLLINS

FANTASTIC

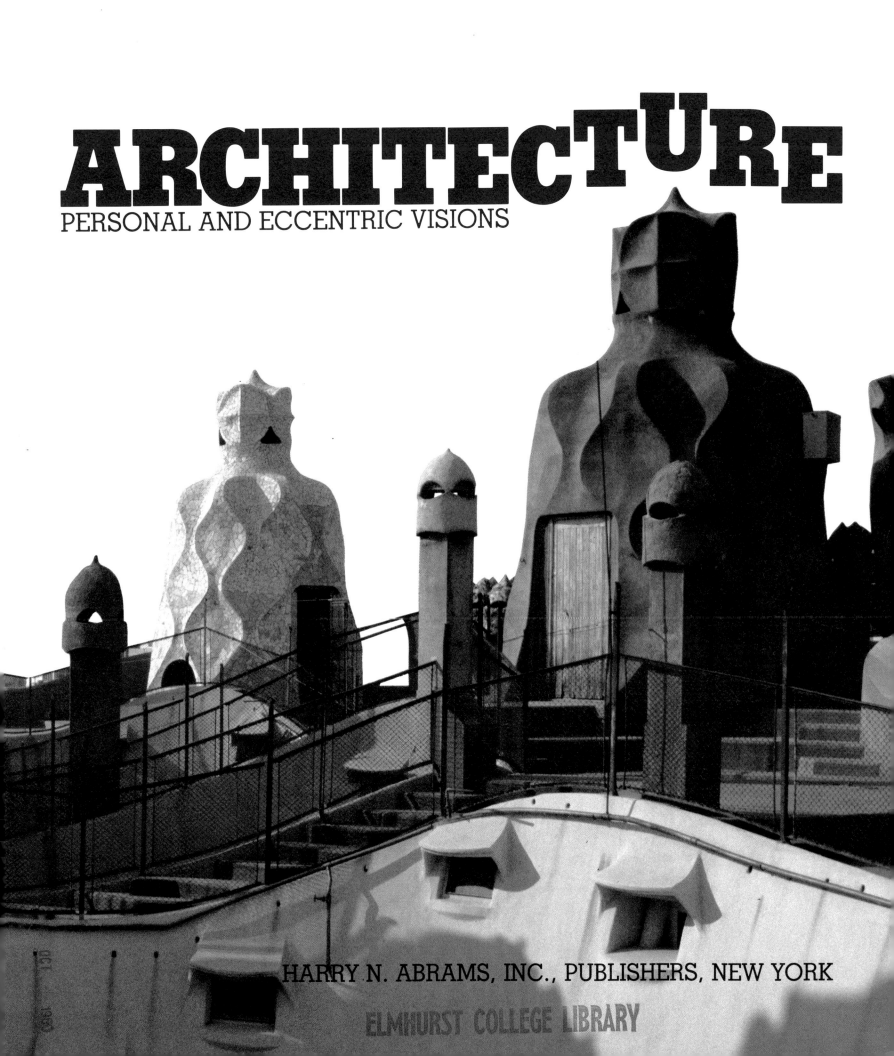

ARCHITECTURE

PERSONAL AND ECCENTRIC VISIONS

HARRY N. ABRAMS, INC., PUBLISHERS, NEW YORK

Half-title page: Hermann Finsterlin, Dream In Glass
Title page: Antonio Gaudí, Casa Milá
Contents page: from Buster Keaton's film One Week

Project Editor: Robert Morton
Editor: Nora Beeson
Designer: Bob McKee

Library of Congress Cataloging in Publication Data

Schuyt, Michael.
  Fantastic architecture.

  1. Grotesque in architecture. 2. Vernacular
architecture.   I. Elffers, Joost, joint author.
II. Collins, George Roseborough, 1917-   III. Title.
NA208.S38   728   80-56
ISBN 0-8109-0914-6

Library of Congress Catalogue Card Number: 80-56

©1980 DuMont Buchverlag, Cologne

All rights for all countries
DuMont Buchverlag GmbH & Co.
Kommanditgesellschaft, Cologne,
Federal Republic of Germany.
The title of the original German edition is:
Phantastische Architektur
George R. Collins/Mike Schuyt/Joost Elffers

CONTENTS

PREFACE

This book and our desire to make it come from a search for information, no, for evidence of an unofficial world of architecture, although "architecture" implies a sense of structure that most of these creations deny. Our aim was to depict the work of architects, artist philosophers, eccentrics, and folk artists and the forms they arrived at with complete freedom of fantasy and without any restriction of zoning laws and building codes.

We have traveled all over the world in search of these fantastic forms in architecture. We do not wish to show everything that exists (even if it were possible), since new shapes are born all the time, but wanted to present in this book and in a traveling exhibit a variety of different dreams, ideas, and creations.

It was a journey through dreams-made-tangible, dreams in stone, wood, bottles, junk, and bushes. Often these builders were retired people without any architectural training, naives who expressed or showed themselves by creating a proof of their being, an expression of their thinking, a symbol of their innermost selves.

A castle in Germany built of discarded material

They are eccentrics to their neighbors and sometimes become hermits because in many cases the surrounding world could not accept them, thus resulting in aggression or total ignorance. Here are some reactions from neighbors who were asked by a photographer about Watts Towers in California. To one, it was a landmark, meaning that he could find his way home when he was drunk. During wartime, a second neighbor suspected that there was a spy ring going on, and he called the F.B.I. The third neighbor, just down the street, had never seen it.

Today many of our generation feel that they have lost touch with the place they live in and have also lost the touch or will to build their own surroundings. An elite of tastemakers seems to have forgotten that a society cannot be organized along lines of enforced growth, that in fact a natural way of life, including the freedom of fantasy, is the only possible way for an individual to form his own free nature and follow his needs.

Michael Schuyt
Joost Elffers

7

FANTASTIC

PART I

Architectural fantasy manifests itself in many ways. It is often spectacular, but it is not easy to categorize and analyze. Perhaps that is what fantastic means: to be so exciting or strange as to be indescribable.

The fantastic can be fun, although I do not think it necessarily is so. Yet it can be a joy both to observe and do. There used to be a slangy term "fantastic" that was interjected to mean either "Oh, boy!" or "How strange!" Here we will see that the fantastic ranges from the most complex utopian and technological visions of our high culture to the day-to-day or weekend-to-weekend hobbies of ordinary folk who like to build, tinker, or shape things for themselves in whatever spare time they have.

Fantastic architecture as represented in this book comprises much that is more important for the way it jolts, excites, or intrigues the eye and mind than for any complete panorama it might offer about anything other than what all sorts of people everywhere do rather randomly. We are not, for the most part, dealing with the central activities of culture in our day nor with those persons who call the signals in it. We are looking largely at fringe figures, but they do make us feel that it would be fun to be there at the fringe with them. Nor is that fringe the frontier of art. They are not so much demonstrating in what direction the arts should go as what a lark it is to do as they do—only differently.

ARCHITECTURE ^{BY GEORGE R. COLLINS}

Fantastic architecture. What the fantastic is we will discuss further on. And what, then, is architecture?

Different times and peoples have had differing ideas about this. Some seem not to have thought much about it at all, but have just built. Others, such as the ancient Egyptians, even deified an early builder and therefore must have had a rather elevated regard for the calling as consisting of leaders of men and culture. Classical civilizations such as the Greek and Roman, and the European Renaissance gave considerable thought to the meaning and function of the professional "architect." "The architect," wrote Vitruvius in Roman times, "should be equipped with knowledge of many branches of study and varied kinds of learning," and he specified the knowledge of history, philosophy, music, medicine, law, astronomy, optics, architecture, as well as possession of talent and the ability to draw well.

In the Middle Ages, the designers of important structures were merely "master masons." Their skilled leaders seem to have been members of secret societies of a powerful, but as yet little understood, nature that were displaced professionally by architects' academies in the Renaissance, although the secret societies continued, converted into occult movements and radical political parties.

In any case, in the course of the Renaissance architects came to think of themselves as humanists, i.e., as practicing the liberal arts and therefore properly belonging to their intellectual academies. From late Baroque times and down through the nineteenth century, institutes, special curricula and ateliers, and more and more schools were organized for the special training of architects, although with the exponential increase in required types of buildings, the architect was given fewer of the important elements of our built environment to design. Military engineers had already taken over from architects in the design of fortifications during the sixteenth century, leaving the architect to build only those defensive castles for aristocrats that function as palaces or villas, some of which we see in this book. Particularly in the following centuries of large garden layouts, there developed the specialty that we now call landscape architect, which is really a separate and somewhat rival calling of landscapist. The industrial revolution gave birth to the polytechnic institution and its products, the various types of engineers who virtually cut off the architect from the increasing number of industrial or technical structures as well as from much building related to transportation: bridges, highways, tracks, tunnels, and ports.

For all the sensational urbanization that came about during the nineteenth century, with its consequent need for housing and run-of-the-mill community buildings, the architect, despite the increasing apparatus for his preparation and stature, shared fewer building commissions. During that century, a metropolis like London

9

almost quintupled in population, and the number of British cities of 100,000 population jumped from two to thirty. In the United States, still a frontier society, the number of centers of 10,000 in population more than tripled between 1800 and 1850. The great mass of construction that accompanied this growth was, of course, carried out by developers and contractors, trained architects playing a very minimal role as is the case also in our day. Much has been said about the mediocrity and monotony of such building, but rarely has any study been made, as is done photographically in this book, of the desperate attempts by which the inhabitants of these humdrum *barrios* have tried to humanize or personalize the buildings and grounds in which they have been lodged.

Most of the built structures shown in this book were not designed by trained architects, but were put together by craftsmen of various sorts, or by individuals who were anything but architects: businessmen, farmers, clerics, postmen, morticians, for instance. And while there are a number of great and famous architects represented, they are often not doing there what is usually expected of an architect, but are engaged in impracticalities, collages, or *scherzos* such as the princely Bomarzo garden (pp. 216–19).

Within the architectural profession, there is not, however, definite agreement as to whether to be architecture a thing must be built or buildable. Visions or fantasies, such as most of the real architects in this book are engaged in, and which are illustrated in our fourth section, are looked at somewhat askance by the profession. As an historian, I would presume that some visions represent the current aspirations and future course of the architectural profession better than any built structure, school curriculum, or written rhetoric. But a recent large exhibition of drawings of visionary architecture and planning, chosen to illustrate the broad spectrum that there is of such "paper architecture," was severely criticized internationally by a prominent member of the profession, who insisted that the only legitimate visionary drawings of architecture were those of structures that could eventually be executed technically. Nearly all the unbuilt proposals in the present volume would not have passed such scrutiny as architecture.

Are then the *built* structures pictured in this book architecture? That is indeed arguable. Some twenty things represented are not by professional architects but by other artists—some quite famous—who are involved in building. And almost without exception, the types of buildings illustrated are not those usually designed by architects and for which architects have earned the sanctity and regality generally associated with their title:

public buildings, cult edifices, urban public spaces, and town or city planning layouts. Nor do most of the buildings depicted look as if they had had the approval of local planning boards and building departments. Oddly enough, a couple of them, idiosyncratic as they may be, have been declared "landmarks" by city commissions; two of them (pp. 176, 179–81) celebrate famous landmarks in their decorative imagery, and Fred Smith's rather comic Concrete Park in Wisconsin (p. 233) was restored recently and published in the professional periodical *Historic Preservation* (1979). My impression is, however, that many Landmarks Commissions, if presented with photographs of Smith's mosaic-encrusted horses, angels, and Indian chiefs, would merely giggle.

In other words, most of what we have here is extra-curricular, not what is taught in architecture schools, and is only peripherally related to architecture.

One reason that architectural ideas are sometimes not considered really to be architecture is that as projects, they never get built, even if feasible. This is, for the most part, not a matter of concern with the things illustrated in the present publication, although in some cases the designer's neighbors may have wished that they never had been started in the first place.

Unbuilt architecture results primarily from three different circumstances: the project was not carried out as planned, it was not really intended to be actually constructed, or it was begun but never completed.

As for the first category, apart from the twenty or so professional architects whose works are illustrated here, most of the builder-designers probably did not plan in advance what they were going to do anyway. In fact, that is one of the reasons that the architectural profession would consider so many of the works here to be illegitimate, because they were not carried out according to the preliminary sketches, rendered plans, sections, elevations, and working drawings that architects are trained to draw in school, but were simply knitted together, in many cases out of *objets trouvés*, i.e., junk, instead of materials obtained by order and purchase from lumberyards, kilns, and quarries. To what extent must architecture be a *thought* in advance or simply an *action* taken—*bricolage* as Claude Lévi-Strauss would put it? This is why, in part, it has been so difficult for anyone to get firm data about builders and works such as this book illustrates.

Virtually all the unbuilts in this volume are of the second category: never really intended to be constructed either because they were drawn up as generalized, prototypical models that would have to be modified for local usage, or because they were a prophetic vision for some future time. Christo's pyramid of oil drums (p. 55) might be thought of as the former type, but nearly all our unbuilts are of the latter type and are to be found in the visionary section of the book. The fact that the visionary part, from Paolo Soleri on, consists almost entirely of built structures is indeed a problem that must be discussed in connection with those projects. In a sense they are built unbuilts.

As regards the third category of unbuilt, begun but not as yet—or ever—really underway, I think there are no examples here. The very opposite is true: many of the projects were building over a rather long period of time and were only terminated, if at all, because their builder abandoned them for one reason or another, including death; it is precisely this quality of continuum in them that makes them so interesting and fantastic.

There is actually a tricky sort of unbuilt in addition to the three categories already discussed, namely buildings that, being painted in *trompe-l'oeil* perspective, appear to be there but actually are not or at least not in that form. Architects would probably consider these to be only decoration, not really architecture (pp. 190–95).

What we have, then, throughout most of this book is not architecture. If so, what should we call it? Nonarchitecture? But most of it is built. "*Architecture douce*" (soft architecture), as a French journal labels it? But for sure it is not soft, and this involves analogy to the French "*énergie douce*," meaning low tech, which is elusive to the English-speaking reader. Folk architecture? Perhaps, but let us explore that term because some of the most folksy-looking structures herein have been produced by highly sophisticated artists like the Saint Phalle team. Vernacular? But a lot of it is not done in a local patois and is not recognizable as specifically British, French, German, gringo, or Yankee, as we shall see.

Architecture d'Aujourd'hui, the French periodical, says:

Soft architecture...refuses to use the processes of production, industrial procedures, and division of labor.... That is, soft architecture tries to establish new relationships between producer and user (often the same person). It is involved in new relations between Man and Nature in its respect for ecosystems, and its refusal to squander energy and materials; it pursues autonomy. It proposes itself as a possibility of poetic expression and total realization which permits an individual to recover his integrity by nonspecialized work, rejecting any division between the intellectual and manual.

In its methods of production it must be artisan, and for obvious reasons it is often self-built; it replaces the project about space-making by the process of space-making; it wishes to be antimonumental, not rhetorical, but poetic.

This is, indeed, what is here illustrated, and furthermore the periodical suggests that this is especially developed in the United States. It is true that more than one-quarter of all the projects in this book are American, the French themselves coming next and comprising one-fifth of the works. No other country comes close, although this is not uniquely an American phenomenon. The periodical does consider that soft architecture rejects the greatest advances of industrialized capitalism, reverts to idealistic and liberal individualism, and is essentially antiurban.

What we have, then, either self-consciously or unconsciously reflects an ideology, and merely from this we know it not to be traditional folk, or vernacular, or anonymous architecture as the substratum of all building everywhere is called.

There is a growing literature on folk architecture; it discusses buildings that do not look like ours in this book. Folk architecture fits into or otherwise acknowledges its site. It is environmental in the sense that it is walled, roofed, windowed, and doored to fit its climatic and social conditions. Its materials and building methods are traditional, regional, and often ethnic. It is not anticapitalist-industrial, but is either pre-such or slightly reflective of more "advanced" technologies if and when they are at its builder's disposal. While it may have been built all or in part by its owner/dweller, one senses that there must have been vernacular architects in the region who function like medieval master masons and retain by custom (not on paper) the regional traditions to which each house and barn, etc.—although a bit different from any other and hence giving variety to the streetscape or landscape—essentially adheres.

There exists a handful of exceptional and interestingly illustrated studies of these matters by architects. A fairly early explorer of the field was Sibyl Moholy-Nagy in her *Native Genius in Anonymous Architecture* of 1957. In keeping with the Bauhaus background of herself and her husband Laszlo, she did indeed underscore the ingenious, adaptive character of folk building. "Buildings," she wrote, "are transmitters of life. They transmit the life of the past into the lives of the future."

Bernard Rudofsky, especially in a memorable exhibition at the Museum of Modern Art in New York City in 1964–65 and in two books, *Architecture Without Architects* for that exhibit, and a follow-up, *The Prodigious Builders* of 1977, illustrated a far greater variety of types—including man burrowing into the ground—and he stressed the dramatic, unusual, and bizarre (i.e., fantastic) qualities of worldwide building that has since time immemorial largely been ignored by students of man's constructional activities. Rudofsky has been an eye-opener. Man has responded directly to environmental conditions, producing prodigious complexes, especially for housing, that are fascinating in appearance.

Amos Rapaport, although an architect, has been more anthropological. His *House Form and Culture* of 1969 indicates how indigenous house forms reflect the subtleties of widely differing cultures. With respect to his analysis of the vernacular, it should be pointed out that in addition to the recognition of such environmental determinants as climate, society, and materials, he stresses the desire of the builders to get their edifices lined up with the stars and heavens: "The cosmos may be reflected in a microcosm at a whole range of scales, from an entire land through a city, a village, a house as a whole, the space within a house, and the furniture in it. Each, or all, may reflect the shape in which the world is visualized."

The British architect Paul Oliver has edited several superb anthologies of studies on vernacular building, often stressing the semiotic aspects of folk culture.

Vernacular building is basically rational—even if apparently unthinking and rather simple in appearance—in the ways that it responds to a variety of circumstances and beliefs. But I repeat, the illustrations in these publications do not look like ours for reasons that *Architecture d'Aujourd'hui* points out so succinctly. For instance, the architect Carlos Flores of Madrid has spent a decade studying and photographing folk architecture of the highly idiosyncratic regions of the Spanish peninsula. He has published five large, spectacular volumes on Spanish folk architecture (1973–77) in which no two buildings are massed, textured, or ornamented identically, and yet none shout out in the fantastic way that so many do in this book.

Architects have often dipped into folk architecture in search of "fundamentals" or "common sense" with respect to basic forms. In our century, this has occurred several times because of the simple massing of folkish house forms, as in the Mediterranean region and especially the white stuccoed, planar effect of buildings on the islands there. The Viennese architect Josef Hoffmann, who pioneered in developing the simple masses of the Viennese Secession movement at the turn of our century, in those same years had sketched the folk architecture of Ischia, the island off Italy. Some of Le Corbusier's early sketches as he was moving toward the cubic, volumetric, sheer-surfaced buildings of the International Style were from a trip he took to the Greek Islands where he found such forms in the houses there. Just at the time that the same modern International Style took root in Spain (1929–30), one of its leaders, Fernando García Mercadal, published a small precursor of Carlos Flores' volumes entitled *La Casa Popular en España* (1930), which was filled with illustrations in this mode. And an art magazine in Barcelona in 1933 argued that the new modern movement in architecture, with its human scale, simple flat-sided, stuccoed, painted-in-elementary-colors style of building that had first developed in northern Europe, where architecture is naturally pitch-roofed, complexly ornamented, and somber in tone, was the result of those northern architects traveling in the Mediterranean and vacationing on the Balearic Islands!

This is not a new practice of architects, to dip into the substrata and explore the overlap between folk and elite architecture. The influential Renaissance architect and treatise writer Sebastiano Serlio (1475–1554) composed the first compendium on domestic architecture, subtitled *Different Dwellings from the Meanest Hovel to the Most Ornate Palace*. Admittedly, there are only a few "hovels" in his treatise, but he does start with them, although the dwellings rapidly become more classical in style and rise in elegance to those for the king. Vitruvius, the Roman architect of the first century, started two books of his treatise (Book II on building methods and Book V on the dwelling house) with a discussion of the curious building practices of primitive man and the varying climatic characteristics of folk architecture.

Eugène Viollet-le-Duc, the French medievalist of the nineteenth century, not only arranged exhibitions of characteristic historic dwelling types at the International Exposition at Paris in 1878, but also published an extensive study, *The Habitation of Man in All Ages*, that started off with an imaginary account of early primitive man finding himself and developing building techniques, not unlike the Vitruvian passage. The architect Charles Garnier used this book for the exhibition Habitations Humaines that he installed at the Paris Exposition of 1889. And young Frank Lloyd Wright found the book in his hometown library and devoured it eagerly.

One wonders what impact this new "popular" (soft) architecture will have on high culture. The so-called Postmodern movement is certainly susceptible to its overt symbolism and its elements of realistic representation. The Venturis, innovators in Postmodernism, are a parallel to it in high cultural circles. Charles Jencks, current chronicler of that movement, has just published a book *Bizarre Architecture*. The Walker Art Center in Minneapolis produced an exhibition and substantial catalogue of popular American architecture in 1974, and in the following year a similar exhibition was held at the American Cultural Center in Paris for which the Centre Pompidou distributed a booklet with color slides. In 1977, the architect Jan Wampler published *All Their Own: People and the Places They Build*, representing his travels through the North American continent.

It has been suggested above that projects shown in our book that are not designed by professional architects are a part of "soft" architecture or what is known by sociologists as popular (as opposed to high, elitist) culture. Several questions arise in this regard. It has already been noted that some of the images from popular culture, e.g. by Niki de Saint Phalle and SITE, are actually produced by high-culture artists. Does this really matter so long as we exclaim about them, "Fantastic!"? Another question is whether we can make our higher elitist culture more democratic or make our popular culture more sophisticated. On that, one authority on popular and high culture, Herbert Gans, is pessimistic. The issue seems to go back to the founding of our country: Should we be Federalist (high but representational) or Democratic (low and popular)? How do the high and low in art and culture relate to the representative vs. the democratic in political/social life?

There have been efforts to set up egalitarian situations, or at least to draw random community people into large-scale design efforts in which, even if supervised by members of the high-culture elite, untrained local citizens are helped in planning or decorating public spaces for their own use with functions and symbols that are really meaningful to them.

The architect Lawrence Halprin has pioneered in this sort of program in the United States with his Take-Part Workshops. He has studied the circumstances that in vernacular situations in our own historic past or in primitive cultures led to successful planning and building that possess a quality of timeless charm and appropriateness. Can these circumstances and effects be duplicated, recreated, today?

In the Take-Part Workshops, members of a community are encouraged to immerse themselves with all their senses in the place and environment where the intended project is to be localized. Group leaders from the Halprin team, not necessarily architects, assist by guiding participants through carefully prepared "scores" (design process for Halprin is almost choreography) that lead the participants to a heightened awareness of their surroundings. The results of these group encounters, which may take several days, are then analyzed by the professionals of his team, and the Halprin team then develops the design on the basis of the community input. The community, although untrained professionally, reviews the plans and continues to keep "in touch," definitely not being excluded from aesthetic discussions. This interface between professionalism (high culture) and naiveté (popular culture) is a delicate equilibrium, with formal and legal responsibility resting with the architects.

These recent group design efforts, which were referred to as "participatory planning," certainly are less individualistic and anarchic than many of the illustrations in this book, but the end results are not dissimilar if the advisers of the projects are able to maintain spontaneity of expression on the part of the individuals working with them.

An example of this sort occurred recently on Manhattan's Upper West Side in New York City at the site of the Tomb of General Grant. The Tomb, a not very inventive adaption of what the famous Greek Mausoleum of Halicarnassus was supposed to have looked like, was built in 1897 with funds provided by popular subscription. In recent years, the area, which appears to be part of Riverside Park but is actually administered by the National Park Service of the U.S. Department of the Interior, was being severely vandalized.

David Dame, then Park Service Superintendent of Manhattan Sites, commented:

Gang fights. Rival gangs using the tomb to settle their differences, often with knives. There was heavy graffiti on the tomb itself, beer cans, trash, people using nooks and crannies for bathrooms. So the thing to do at Grant's Tomb was not to build a high fence and hire extra guards, but rather to give the community up there pride of ownership in the site. It's the difference between the island mindset that shuts people out and welcoming them into what, after all, is theirs.

In 1972, the sculptor Pedro Pablo Silva, assisted by the architect Philip I. Danzig and others, was retained by the National Park Service with subsidy from New York's City Arts Workshop to make mosaic designs on the benches around the Tomb as a diversion from vandalism. Over the course of three years the benches were freely shaped in hollow concrete and a team of artists and architects involved local people—adults, children, students, etc.—in covering the concrete benches with tile designs. Figure 1 shows the inventive free forms and spatial qualities of the new construction. To judge from spontaneous public events that take place at the Tomb—

1. Benches at Grant's Tomb, New York City

2. Paired houses, Jersey City, New Jersey

and they are increasingly occurring there especially in summertime—the people lounge about on the benches as if at home, and vandalism has been minimal to the benches themselves.

Although we will see that the artistic techniques, materials, etc., employed on the Grant Tomb benches are superficially (as regards their surfaces) similar to mosaic materials employed by designers in this book, there is, of course, a difference between individualistic design bits being melded into a communal whole—however "popular" it may be as expression—and the isolated individual, sometimes rural, efforts which are documented in our book.

It is interesting, and we have already noted, that there has been a tendency to identify "soft" architecture, or pop-building, with the United States. It seems to have accelerated since World War II and represents, at least in part, the activity of workers who have been retired by the social system. We can see this in the large trailer towns of the West Coast, whose trailers actually never move and are surrounded by hummingbird feeders and the like. It is a somewhat desperate situation. In big cities like New York, on a sunny day, the crowds on the sidewalks of the commercial, financial districts, chatting and eating snacks, are not only office workers from upstairs, but also recent retirees who, bored, have commuted in at noon from their suburban homes to hang around on the sidewalks with their buddies as they used to on their lunch hour. But the retirees in our book (from bakeries, businesses, government, clothing and shoe stores, schools, and the like) are not compulsive commuters but rather homebodies like stamp collectors and other hobbyists. They want to heighten the interest of their own territories, inside and out, and will spend long hours, days, weeks, months, and years at it until they themselves leave us—leaving something behind for us that is individually theirs and not of a family or region of indeterminate date, as with folk architecture.

Although some of the designer-builders, whose work is pictured here, choose to remain anonymous, their art is usually quite friendly and neighborly. Although they do not, as we have stressed, design the open public spaces of high culture, their work is not fenced off from others or museum-contained (although museums have lately been exhibiting them, like Grandma Moses).

They are spontaneously democratic.

But to return to the title *Fantastic Architecture*. What *is* meant by "fantastic" as it applies to building?

The *Oxford English Dictionary* has some rather obscurely differentiated definitions of the word "fantastic," one being that of eccentric or extravagant fancy, which certainly does apply adjectively to the many astounding things pictured in this book. But the dictionary also relates the adjective "fantastic" to the noun "fantasy," or rather "phantasy," a more directly imaginative or visionary conception. In this sense it is spelled with "ph," thus approximating the original ancient Greek usage of the word. Phantasy has something to do with the *mental* process of sensuous perception of things that are not actually present, i.e., visionary. Now the visionary has played a considerable role in architectural conceptualizing in all times, even when architecture as such did not exist and despite the reservations of some authorities that are mentioned above. In general, the visionary represents a theoretical, speculative, or even poetic statement or position that is likely to be considerably ahead of its time and may not even be intended to be carried out. It is, then, prophetic, utopian, and in our century often technological to the point of being science fiction. This is obviously a very "architectural" matter and is illustrated in "The Visionaries."

How, then, does "phantasy" apply to the rest of the examples, if at all, since they are often of the character of a popular culture that is more concerned with acting out the present or reminiscing romantically about the past than predicting the future? Most architectural phantasies or visions exist only on paper as drawings. But can there not be a more popular or vernacular form of phantasy and vision that cannot be drawn because the person phantasizing does not know how to draw? Such an idea takes on an actually built form, although still being almost pure phantasy, pure fiction, but right there where you can see it, like a silent movie. It is produced by someone who is not an architect, so it is not really architecture and is not high or elite enough to be art. It is also not art because it has no describable or recognizable style; vernacular or folk architecture has style, which, although it does not tend to change much with the passage of time, still has a describable consistency about it.

We have, then, works that are not simply extravagant, eccentric, and grotesque, but are physical (not merely mental) representations of things not actually present, i.e., built bizarre visions. I stress this because we do actually find, in studying a city of today, houses that predict in a visionary way the direction in which design is moving. This is not done by sketching or drawing, but by buildings having become the way they want to be.

A researcher and photographer of such changes in metropolitan New York, Camilo Vergara, became fascinated with what he was seeing in streets of free-standing or attached—usually frame—houses in various areas, some badly devastated, in the New York region. Adjacent and paired structures that were originally identical are individually transformed (Fig. 2). Was this a creative act such as was done by Marcel Dhièvre (pp. 179–81) or in Dives-sur-Mer (p. 183)? In other words, there are elements of the phantastic, and at times even the visionary, that appear along a commonplace street in a residential quarter. Alerted to this, one will notice it in driving past many American towns and cities, especially where an Interstate highway has bisected an old residential quarter.

We illustrate only a single pair of houses; in many cases the changes are merely textural or coloristic and not as dramatically different as here. Sometimes it is one or two houses standing out in a strip, sometimes a rainbowlike spectrum spilling along a considerable distance, and sometimes a small isolated clump trying to hold its own in a large area of total devastation. Vergara has set up a team including a sociologist, an architectural historian, and an art historian (his wife) to study this.

Sometimes the home improvement work is done by the owner and/or resident with materials that are found or are surplus at their place of employment—in which case the result may be as bizarre as other examples in this book. In other instances a contractor is hired, or sells himself, and an economically efficient product is used for siding, new facing, dormers, turrets, and the like. These streetscapes and individual houses change in appearance from year to year. The process is a dynamic, continuous one as Vergara's time-lapse photographs reveal. In the first stage, as in the house on the left in Fig. 2, the intent is to remove damaged, dangling, and dangerous parts of the building, producing a stripped-down effect that some owners think is "modern." But as we see in Fig. 2, right, neighbors may go on to more picturesque embroideries.

The question that Vergara's team is trying to answer is what are the basic motivations here. Is it individualism, a class structure, ethnic tastes, or other? Is there a universal underlying reason? Is it a new process or is it only that we had not taken notice of it before? It certainly represents the action of individual householders as opposed to residents of large housing complexes, but is it a *statement* of the former against the latter? Is it incipient suburbanism? How much is it pure fantasy or phantasy?

When interviewed, the owners nearly always stress the simple practical reasons for their choices. For instance, Mrs. Mazola of Brooklyn said: "The whole top fell in; we had to fix it!" She opted for bondstone facing. "But who wants aluminum siding [which her semi-detached neighbor used on the second floor]? Everything functions in this house; things not necessary are ridiculous." Compared with what has been said earlier about regenerating life after retirement, this may be a desperate familial attempt to hold or regenerate a neighborhood or community.

Is the material illustrated here avant-garde?

Some is, some is not. Most of the works pictured in "The Artists," and some of that in "The Visionaries" is—or was in its day—avant-garde, but most of the rest is not.

The nature of the avant-garde in art, architecture, and building has been considerably discussed, especially in recent years, and it has been determined that the expression arose in the early mid-nineteenth century in France to describe the anti-establishment, prophetic character of certain artist/writer groups and movements. The term itself is a military one, comparable to the British "vanguard." As the *Random House Dictionary of the English Language* notes: "The advance group in any field, especially in the visual, literary, or musical arts, whose works are characterized chiefly by unorthodox and experimental methods." As it has come to be employed in the arts, the term avant-garde does not actually correspond to its military analogy because what we have described as having occurred in France implies that the avant-garde is not a matter of organized specialists who are leading the pack, but a sort of guerrilla group, loosely held together, that is attacking the main body of its own military force.

But the military term clearly applies to certain distinctions that can be made between works in this book. In an army, the avant-garde consists of a highly trained elite—crack troops—who are way out front, know precisely how their actions relate to the masses, may lead the masses behind them, and make decisions. Folk, vernacular, and popular art are, however, what are called the "other ranks," wedded to tradition, and insofar as the future is concerned, just puttering about. In the art we have in this book, the work is full of reminiscences of "back home," and, like the workshop units of a mobile army, the designers are keeping things together

with the aid of *objets trouvés* in vehicular dumps, as with the construction of the houses of Mike Reynolds (pp. 148–50), Grandma Prisbrey (pp. 156–59), and Fred Burns (p. 171).

This is not to say that paratroopers cannot be inspired to bravery by the sight of close-marching troops. Some of the popular-culture buildings in "Unusual Materials" and "Interiors—Exteriors" seem to have inspired famous artists. These perform in the general style that has been called—appropriately enough—Pop Art. While Pop Art may have more frequently drawn its inspiration from commercial art and illustration, some of those who are included under that designation like Niki de Saint Phalle (or Kurt Schwitters of Dada, a forerunner of Pop Art) do works that are in harmony with "Unusual Materials" and "Interiors—Exteriors."

There remains only one other general statement that I care to make about the character of the works in this book: they are remarkably *colorful*. This not only implies that they are fantastic or striking (colorful in the slangy sense), but also that they are more polychromatic and meaningfully so (symbolically colorful) than most historic architecture—especially high architecture which in "great" periods such as the Greek classic, High Gothic, Roman Baroque, and International Modern style has not been very polychromatic, as has been, say, an Antonio Gaudí (pp. 122–27).

In the past hundred years or so, there has been considerable discussion and controversy in academic and professional circles as to how color should be employed in architectural massing and decoration. After a period of dead white classicism in the late eighteenth century, it was discovered that the ancients had colored parts of their buildings apparently for emphatic symbolic reasons. In the picturesque middle of the nineteenth century, everything went rather painterly and colorful. But the application of color to building in terms of the random hues of found objects employed to put the whole together is pretty much an act of the twentieth century and is to be found primarily in the "naive architecture" of which there are so many illustrations in color in this book.

PART II

The miscellanies of fantastic projects and works have been divided into categories that are not airtight. Nevertheless, they do give us groupings by which we can attempt to comprehend the works. Let us look at these various groups.

1. THE ARTISTS (AND ARCHITECTS)

It is certainly appropriate to lead off with the eighteenth-century figure Giovanni Battista Piranesi (p. 32). He is an archetypal phantast. Having immersed himself in the lost grandeur of the great buildings of ancient Rome, he depicted them graphically again and again, not only slightly distorted for his own purposes (as a modern photographer of the same monuments has demonstrated), but often half-buried in the debris of centuries and serving as the background or lodging for the Romans of Piranesi's day, who seem to have had little comprehension of what they were living in and around. In connection with what has been discussed above, these protrusions of the most massive and elite public buildings of all time are reduced to serve as the structural elements of a modern popular architecture. They cannot, however, be completely vernacularized, anymore than can the boat tilted up for use as a house in Denmark (p. 151) or the whale body serving as a car wash (p. 96).

But in the print illustrated here, one of the bizarre frontispieces to Piranesi's series of volumes *The Antiquities of Rome*, he really deals with popular, "artistic" invention. This is presumably the Appian Way, the famous Roman road stretching over three hundred miles south of the city and flanked at its start with funeral monuments. He has made it look like the work of the Postman Cheval (pp. 66–69) or even Clarence Schmidt (pp. 200, 201) because of the intolerable congestion in build up of cemetery memorials. Apparently this was a true situation in Greek and Roman times when they had, periodically, to clean out such littered public spaces and start all over again.

Actually, the work that in our day most closely approximates Piranesi's effect and intentions is Juan O'Gorman's house in the lava Pedregal of Mexico City (pp. 36, 37). O'Gorman, like Piranesi a totally rational architect, seems to have become so enamored of the odd geology of this volcanic residue on the outskirts of Mexico City that he embroidered and mosaicized it with a myriad of symbolic designs, presumably drawn from ancient pre-Columbian Mexico—just as Piranesi's phantasy is a jumble of ancient Roman bits of architecture, sculpture, furniture, and household utensils.

Edward James appears to have developed a quite different romanticism about pre-Columbian civilizations and their architectures during his decades of building in the forest of Xilitla in Mexico (pp. 32–35). As regards phantasy, perhaps the most exciting thing about the built structures of the ancient American cultures is the act of exploring, finding, and wresting them from the overgrowing vegetation of centuries. To stumble on James's structures would seem to be like discovering another of the mysterious civilizations of Latin America, whose built structures are so monumental and so like things we have seen elsewhere in the ancient world that we immediately dream up diffusionist cultural hypotheses, avant-garde scouting parties on transoceanic rafts, or worlds in collision in order to explain what, as with Edward James, may have been quite spontaneously inventive right there.

Robert Tatin in France (pp. 44, 45) and Bruno Weber in Switzerland (pp. 46–49) are, although more figurative in their forms, somewhat similar in the abundance of their primitive symbolic, apparently magical or demonic, imagery. But unlike Piranesi and James, they cannot draw on preceding times in their own lands—which produced nothing remotely like what they do—but rather they seem to derive from popular ideas of primitive or oriental, i.e., exotic traditions.

Another way to phantasize is to dwell on monstrous, nightmarish images that combine gargantuan size with an occasional touch of porn. This is to be seen in the works by Niki de Saint Phalle and her team (pp. 38–40, 52–54).

Kurt Schwitters in his day—the 1920s and 30s—was one of our greatest masters of collage, producing decorative surfaces of a variety of found and scissored objects, always witty in the juxtaposition of symbolic elements. His *Merzbau* construction within his own house (p. 43) was essentially a multidimensional collage that contained within it a number of what he called "grottoes," in which he had installed objects. Schwitters himself said about the construction, which he purposely never finished but always kept working on:

The building grows somewhat according to the regulations of a metropolis, in which, in each case that a new house is supposed to be added somewhere, the building supervisor must see to it that the new house does not ruin the cityscape. So I find some object, I realize that it belongs to this sculpture, I take it with me, stick it on, paste it up, paint it in the rhythm of the total effect, and one day it will become apparent that some new tendency must be created which will go in some way beyond the dead body of the object.

As opposed to the rather modest dimensions of Schwitters, Christo (p. 55) and Jim Turrell (pp. 50, 51) are of the Space Age, manipulating structures and covering the surface of the earth itself on a scale that makes even the Pyramids of Egypt seem diminutive. In both cases they strain the limits of human comprehension, creating constructs that cannot be taken in or apprehended by a glance unless it be from a position in the skies—from which art has seldom, if ever, been designed before.

And, finally, Salvador Dali (p. 41) fits into no specific category, believing himself to be the ultimate phantast of all time.

2. CASTLES AND TOWERS

In the world of phantasy, castles and towers embrace quite a range of constructions from the actual to imitations, on different scales, and in varied materials. Towers may or may not be castellated in effect. Also included is an excavated structure on the grounds of a castle, made to imitate a real cave, and capable of serving as a habitable space—i.e., a grotto.

The historic castlelike buildings shown are of remarkably different character. The earliest, one built for the Prince of Palagonia (pp. 59–61, 192–93) in 1715, is really more of a villa of late Baroque design, with dramatic decorations of weird figures and illusionistic frescoes. Romantic Goethe did not miss visiting it during his Sicilian trip of 1787. Next, chronologically, is one of the several castles of Ludwig II, the "Dream King" of Bavaria. His royal retreat at Neuschwanstein was designed in 1869 by the stage painter Christian Jank on the basis of plans drawn up by the architect Eduard Riedel. A few years later a Wagnerian Grotto was designed for Neuschwanstein, but then transferred by the "Mad" King to his castle at Linderhof and built, as we see it here, by his landscape gardener (pp. 58, 59). It included an artificial underground lake electrically lit.

As regards really functional, fortified castles, that in Beit et Dine, Lebanon (pp. 62, 63), although fancifully decorated earlier in this century as if it were a rural "folly," is very likely now serving as a strong point for the family of one or another of the warring factions involved in what its inscription shouts as "Lebanon forever!"

Who is to say, actually, whether a castle is real or false until it is besieged? But some are definitely more playful than others, especially when not built for aristocrats, their traditional residents. One of the most marvelous, modern castlelike structures was put together over a period of some three decades by the postman-farmhand Ferdinand Cheval in south-central France (pp. 66–69). It

all started, we are told, with a curiously shaped stone on which he had once stumbled in his rounds, took home with him, and then, with it as a cornerstone, began to build an extravaganza of shapes that are largely of oriental inspiration and mostly constructed out of such found objects.

The idea of "castle" seems always to have lent itself to building in imitation materials: "castles in the air," sand castles on the beach, and castles of ice in cold climates. All of these seem exceedingly elusive and transitory when one presumes that historical castles were meant to supply permanence and strong points at times when all else failed in a world awash with nomadic raiders, in periods of classic feudalism, and at the edges of competing religious faiths as with the 10,000 castles in Spain. The world of artificial castle-building is indeed a contradictory one. The Dutch low-tide hobbyist Pieter Wiersma is actually paid in this life to preserve buildings historically, but spends his spare time like a child at elaborate constructions that disappear overnight (pp. 64, 65, 248). The icy Swiss and Canadian castles (pp. 74, 75) melt down as the weather changes, but might in the meantime be habitable.

Towers may or may not be associated with castles, depending on whether they seem to be lookouts, spires, or monuments in their own right. All three types are represented. Most castellated in appearance is the Tower of the Apocalypse, built by Robert Garcet in Belgium (pp. 70–72). That it is a *sacred* fortress is indicated by the four symbols of the Evangelists on its top corners: Man (Matthew), Lion (Mark), Ox (Luke), and Eagle (John). Otherwise Garcet seems either to have taken liberties with the twenty-first chapter of the Book of Revelation, or has used some Catholic commentary on the Apocalypse, such as that of the Spanish eighth-century monk Beatus of Liebana, because, although one is accustomed to associate sheep and lambs with the faith, large dragons do not figure, the inscriptions are not from the scriptures, and even that phantast St. John writing on the Island of Patmos in our first century could hardly have imagined tanks and rocket projectiles (p. 72). Also, what God's angel revealed to John in the Apocalypse was not actually a single tower, but the Holy Jerusalem lying there foursquare like its godchild, Salt Lake City, Utah. As revealed to St. John, it had twelve gates, often depicted as towered in medieval manuscripts of the Apocalypse, each gate with an angel, and the twelve corresponding to the twelve tribes of Israel and to the twelve Apostles of the Lamb—but not to the four Evangelists. Furthermore, the idea of a single tower in Early Christian lore and writings seems not to be associated with the Holy Jerusalem but with the

Tower of Babel (i.e., Babylon, the evil city of Man), a structure of multiple meanings and a prototype for our twentieth-century towering projects for megastructures, themselves a phantastic idea.

Ed Galloway's Oklahoma phantasy (pp. 72, 73) is, as a tower, more of a folly, enterable and inscribed rather than castellated.

And, finally, Sam Rodia's famous Watts Towers in Los Angeles (pp. 78–81) are seemingly spires of a non-existent cathedral and as such—in part because of the broken-tile appliqué—have frequently been compared to Antonio Gaudí's Sagrada Familia church in Barcelona (pp. 122, 123), with which they have, actually, nothing to do at all.

3. Ice-cream stand as freezer, Massachusetts

3. BUILDINGS AS...

If the first habitations of man were caves or simply bent boughs, there is really no reason why, historically, buildings should have any set appearance or that a house should necessarily look like a house as it is commonly known in the Western world. In fact, after leafing through Rudofsky's *The Prodigious Builders*, one is not quite sure what even a "traditional" building looks like, because man has employed so many structures and shapes in order to escape the weather and the spirits and to go about his business sheltered.

We are not, however, concerned with vernacular oddities but rather with the intentional casting of buildings into shapes that symbolize, rather than functionalize, their use. This is usually done for simple commercial or advertising reasons, comparable to what Robert Venturi refers to as a "duck," but on occasions this vulgar exploitative shaping has edged up into the high and abstract *art* of architecture and can symbolize a social/philosophical principle. Such was the case with the eighteenth-century French Romantic Classic architects Ledoux, Boullée, Lequeu, and Barbier who appear in various guises throughout the illustrations (pp. 84–87, 102, 103, 175, 243). The philosophers of the French Enlightenment evolved various utopian theories of living, for which their architects tried to design appropriate structures. One idea of appropriateness involved a sort of symbolic functionalism in which the building was *shaped* so as to indicate an important aspect of its purpose. Called *architecture parlante* (speaking architecture), it is clear from this section of the book that the concept has never really left us.

Ledoux's workshop for a cooper (p. 103) seems to be composed of hoops, and his house for a director of waterworks (unillustrated) was to be shaped like a pipe with a stream of water gushing through it. Boullée's Cenotaph

4. Houseboat, Amsterdam

(funeral monument) for Sir Isaac Newton (p. 102) gives the effect of stars in the sky to those inside it during the daytime, but would be lit at night by a complicated astronomical instrument called an armillary sphere (actually a skeletal celestial globe). The Oikema, or Temple Dedicated to Love (p. 86)—for Ledoux's ideal city of Chaux, which was to be laid out so as to function according to the social principles of Jean-Jacques Rousseau—is in plan a phallus, although that organ is appropriately concealed to the outside world by the tailoring of the building's exterior, which is not at all phallic in shape. As Ledoux wrote about this design:

Here one abandons himself to the torrents of counterfeit pleasures dashing along toward destruction.... Having lured the impetuous and fickle youths, the Oikema confronts them with the starkest deprivation; but the feeling of degradation of man rekindles sleeping virtue, and leads man to the altar of virtuous Hymen, who embraces and crowns him.

This building, then, was placed there in order to educate the city's youth *out* of the pleasures of the brothel, which it was.

The types of building represented include foodstand, restaurant, gas station, latrine, pavilion, car wash, office building, institution, but primarily the house. The structures are cast in a wide variety of representational shapes. Foods: the hot dog and the cake. Plants: the mushroom and the pineapple. Creatures: the snail, horse, cow, elephant, and whale. Apparel: the shoe, boot, and hat. Also, the covered wagon, bulldozer, boat, broken column, and barrel. In other sections we see faces (p. 41), the female body (p. 54), and groves of trees (p. 175).

That a house is designed in the form of an animal, like an elephant, is not necessarily a joke (p. 92); this building, sometimes called a hotel, is still today in Margate City just south of Atlantic City, New Jersey, having been built in 1883 after a patent taken out by a J. V. Lafferty the previous year. It cost some $38,000 to erect, according to a leaflet describing it, employing a million pieces of timber, four tons of bolts, etc., and 12,000 square feet of tin in construction. A later, larger one with three stories of rooms in it was constructed at Coney Island, New York City, but lasted only until 1896. Stairs are in the rear legs of the pachyderm.

Houses built as shoes are not infrequent, perhaps because of the children's tale. There was, for instance, another shoe-house constructed in York, Pennsylvania, by a shoe manufacturer, apparently designed in part to demonstrate the easily plastic qualities of solid, poured concrete.

But examples of *architecture parlante* can outlive their meaning. We illustrate an example of this: an ice-cream stand that used to be on a strip along a highway in western Massachusetts was constructed in the form of a gigantic ice-cream freezer (Fig. 3)—a mechanism that is not used anymore to churn out that particular American delicacy and hence would be unrecognizable today to the very youths that it was designed to attract.

Houses especially take on other than house forms, not for reasons of symbolic expression but merely out of desperation or even "squatting," i.e., in order to reside without having to buy or rent an expensive plot of land. Boats are, of course, classic refuges for such people, and we find permanent residences to be as common throughout marinas as in trailer parks. Amsterdam has, however, a special twist on this. On its canals there are several thousand barges set up as residences (Fig. 4) not only for folk, but also for pets, gardens, etc. Such a barge-as-house is connected to a power line and water supply, and the dweller in it is subject to various municipal regulations. It has been suggested that this use of barges for houses in Amsterdam was influenced by Chinese living in junks, although living in barges that actually travel and work has long been common to commercial waterways and canals all over the world.

Certainly one of the most colorful marinas anywhere is that in Sausalito, California, across the bay north of San Francisco (pp. 208, 209). Here designers have carried the matter of living in a boat or ship further by turning the superstructures into architectural phantasies, including one called The Madonna that had the effect of a cathedral both inside and out. A recent pictorial anthology of the most lived-in marinas throughout the world is Mark Gabor's *House Boats* (1979).

Boats built up like pagodas or churches are one thing, but buildings looking like boats are another. In some cases the buildings—frequently houses—are so boatlike that one wonders if boat hulls have actually been recycled into them, or at least used to begin their construction (pp. 98, 99). In one case, in Antwerp, the great seaport, the balcony of a house (p. 203) looks as if a retired sea captain had built it from the prow of a favorite sailing vessel.

The fact that modern buildings designed under the influence of the architect Le Corbusier have marine lines is not unusual. For Georges-Henri Pingusson, who was very close to the master, the reason may have been that the ocean liner was among the twentieth-century machines to which Le Corbusier likened architecture in his theoretical writings. In Le Corbusier's *Ville Radieuse* (*The Radiant City*) of 1933, he printed both a side elevation and a cross section of a large ocean liner, calling it in one case "this floating city" and in the other "a floating apartment house." He said: "I suggest we moor a tired liner on one of our new housing developments as a demonstration of *what can be done!*" So it is no wonder that at a sharp street corner an apartment house might have a prow (p. 98). But such marine appearance has also characterized many early modern buildings of French extraction simply as a stylism. This is certainly true in Latin America where in Lima, Peru, whole streets of modern houses have a distinctly marine cast, especially in their balconies that have iron pipe railings and overhang like a ship's bridge. The fashionable seashore restaurant Miramar in Viña del Mar, Chile, looks for all the world like a ship's superstructure stranded on the rocks.

Another exotic house form, very popular in our day, is the motor van (Fig. 5), a "gypsy" affair. Americans are probably the most nomadic people in the modern world and in that respect seem never to have been equaled, even by the Mongols. Not only do American families easily uproot themselves and move to another part of the United States, but we have those who migrate seasonally, like shepherds and their flocks, between Florida and New England, as well as city dwellers who migrate every summer to beach houses at a great distance. So well equipped for transients are the outskirts of our towns that some years ago a writer in the *Architectural Review* of London observed that a car owner in the United States can live out his life without ever entering a city center, except perhaps for some needed document, but certainly not to shop. With a van in which they can actually *live*, the occupants are almost completely self-sufficient and can cruise from one strip-caravanserai to another.

In the decoration of their mobile homes, however, the owners of American vans seldom equal the truck drivers of the Middle East (Fig. 6). Presumably the driver of this vehicle has another home or caravanserai when he is not on the road, but the attention he has bestowed on his vehicle certainly suggests which place of rest is the most important to him. This is a Pakistan truck, typical of those slogging it out on the new Karakoram Highway that is being cut from Pakistan into western China.

5. *"Ballroom Blitz" van*

6. *Pakistan truck*

4. THE VISIONARIES

Visionaries represent a major contribution to the world of phantasy if only because, as designers of the future, they seldom have to *build* their visions. This is not to say that they are irresponsible, but the fact is that they certainly can give vent to their wildest dreams.

Visionaries are drawn from all walks of life: artists, architects, laymen, social theorists, and faddists all press their visionary schemes on the public, although we

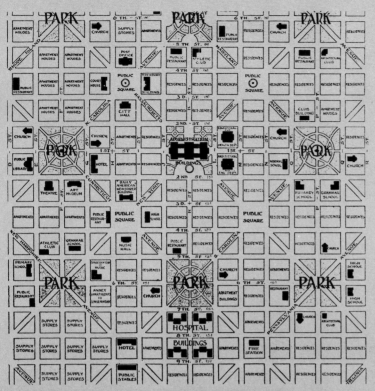

7. *City plan from* The World as a Department Store, *1900*

8. *Nicolai A. Ladovsky, Maison commune, 1919*

are here limited, of course, to those concepts that have been given unusual visual form. The visions have been arranged in this book by formal type and aesthetic character. It might be worthwhile to sort them out a bit as regards their purposes.

To begin with, there are some projects that are not ordinarily thought of as visionary. Take the oldest one, for instance, the eighteenth-century observatory in Jaipur, India (pp. 118–20). Although its forms have always been admired for their phantastic shapes, the intention of the Maharaja's constructions at Jaipur and elsewhere was presumably a scientific pursuit of accurate measurement—not exactly an imaginary statement ahead of its time, which we presume the visionary to be. On the other hand, astronomy, one of the oldest and most mystic of sciences, was already worked into all sorts of abstract world systems by the Greek philosophers and was included in the Quadrivium of instruction in the Middle Ages along with arithmetic, geometry, and music. Furthermore, throughout history compelling desires of astronomers have always been, on the one hand, to get their earthly constructions into some sort of harmony with celestial bodies (the clock was apparently invented not to tell time but as a model of planetary motion), and, on the other hand, in astrology, to foretell future events and occurrences by study of the positions of sun, moon, planets, and stars. In this sense, what the Maharaja built, while not visionary in itself, may have had as ultimate purpose one of these visionary pursuits of traditional astronomy.

Another set of nonvisionary projects is the work of SITE—Sculpture in the Environment, Inc. (pp. 134–37). I have myself worked closely enough with this team to know that it is indeed idealistically motivated. In these projects that its members have devised and carried out, however, they are being essentially pranksters, like some of the tongue-in-cheek theorists of the past decade (pp. 106, 107, 116, 117). What SITE is predicting in its "visions" is essentially what we, and presumably they, hope will never come about. How, then, should we view these works? Are they to be savored like the scherzo movement in a long symphony, telling us with musical and/or architectural wit to relax from our serious concentration on things; or are they millennial doomsday warnings like a tympanum of the Last Judgment over the door of a medieval cathedral, saying that everything earthly will indeed fall to pieces like this and we should wait and pray for the other nonmaterial world to come. Much visionary art is ambiguous, and perhaps for that reason SITE belongs.

A matter mentioned earlier is that of unbuilt vs. built visions. It is usually assumed that visionary architecture is paper architecture with the exception of certain technological visions that later prove can be carried out, as the Biblical Tower of Babel was realized in the American skyscraper. However, just about half of the visions illustrated are built structures. Basically, the reason a built structure is not thought to be visionary is that even if the original projects and drawings are quite phantastic and futuristic, the end result would be much diluted because of the intervention of ordinances, customs, contractors, material limitations, patronage difficulties, and even time itself.

Nevertheless, there have been in this world from time to time, and especially in the modern period, certain designers of visions who, like Michelangelo or Bernini, have been able to associate so closely with the construction process as to produce something that can be even *more* visionary and phantastic than their original sketched projects. That is certainly the case with Antonio Gaudí (pp. 122–27), Rudolf Steiner (pp. 128–30), Eric Mendelsohn (p. 131), and Paolo Soleri (pp. 110–13), all of whom have operated with such singular *artistic* genius that the built results in their cases are as visionary and prophetic (whether or not their prophecies are ever realized) as their original intentions. Also, in studying their works we realize that we are reading a highly subjective *autobiography*, even if none of them has ever actually written such a chronicle. Their built works are, then, highly indicative of what they, personally, feel the world should aspire to. And in the case of Gaudí, it can be demonstrated that each successive building that he constructed in this century was actually a visionary project for his next one to come. I say this because a study of his drawings for building indicates that each drawing for a new building is derived from the edifice he had just built, but the drawing does not look much like the building the drawing was intended for, because Gaudí would radically change the project in many ways as it was built under his personal supervision. This is the case with all four of his projects illustrated here, but will not be so with the Passion facade (pp. 122, 123) of the Sagrada Familia church, which is being copied from his drawings by his successors.

A basic distinction that might be made is between different types of vision such as the social and the technological. The social visionary is a utopian—very characteristic of the nineteenth century—postulating cure-alls for society and very often providing little visual representation, or at least any visual material interesting enough for inclusion here. The architectural elements of a social vision are often humdrum. The technological visionary, especially in our century, is quite the opposite, given to phantasy like science fiction and often committed to the belief that technological progress will cure social problems. Such an attitude is

somewhat in eclipse today, but it did flourish a generation ago—witness Le Corbusier's image of the city as an efficient ocean liner, a machine that has now usually been scrapped or tied up in a marina like an oversized "Madonna" of Sausalito.

Primary example of a utopian vision here and underway is the Auroville commune near Pondicherry in India (p. 121). It appears also to be appreciably phantastic with its jeweled ellipsoid central structure of presumed cosmological meaning. Utopias are, however, not necessarily of as high elite culture as this one, but they may rather be an expression of the popular culture that has béen discussed above. For instance, in the millennial year of 1900 there was published in Lewiston, Maine, an unusually low-key and "practical" utopian tract entitled *The World as a Department Store; a Story of Life under a Cooperative System* and "dedicated to the suffering toilers of all walks of life." In a novelesque fashion common to utopian tracts of that day, the hero has fallen asleep for a quarter of a century to awake in a world totally reorganized according to the ideals of the author Bradford Peck, himself president of the largest department store in New England outside of Boston. The major buildings drawn as illustrations for the book are in conventional Beaux Arts taste, looking much like the World's Columbian Exposition of 1893 and therefore totally understandable to their public. Peck's plan for his new, efficiently organized city (Fig. 7) has just that quality of introducing formal order into the chaotic American city-spread of the day needed to entice the layman to his scheme. A nuts-and-bolts vision that is fun—like many of the houses pictured here.

The technological visions in our book are indeed phantastic ones of the Space Age. Buckminster Fuller has suggested that great translucent orbs can float about in the atmosphere by virtue of the sun-warmed air within them being buoyant in relation to that outside them (p. 104). Thomas Shannon has proposed, instead, hovering islands in the air (pp. 104, 105), reminding one of Paul Scheerbart's novel *The Emperer of Utopia* (1904), in which houses, restaurants, and even cities were to hover, balloon-supported, above the earth for the delight of their residents and customers. And, finally, there is that Princeton professor, Gerard K. O'Neill, to whose space-colony organization every self-respecting visionary belongs, proposing that tubular space cities, whirling to achieve a sense of gravity, can be positioned out there at point Lagrange 5 (where the sun and moon never set) and constructed largely of materials shot there from the surface of the not-so-gravitational moon (p. 108).

Otherwise the projects illustrated are from the best-known visionary periods and circumstances: Ledoux

23

(p. 103), Boullée (p. 102), and Lequeu (p. 102) of the eighteenth-century Romantic Classicists discussed above and of renown especially for Ledoux's elaborate project for the Royal Salt Works in the forest of Chaux at Arc-en-Senans in France—a portion of which was actually carried out. Of the German Expressionists, the unbuilt visions of Wassili Luckhardt (p. 100), Hermann Finsterlin (p. 115), and Bruno Taut (p. 114) are represented, as well as a built structure of Eric Mendelsohn (p. 131), and associated with the movement in this particular project, Kurt Schwitters. Of the marvelous Suprematist/Constructivist projects of the early Soviet period, a curious one is included by Nikolai Aleksandrovich Ladovsky, leader of the ASNOVA group and a prominent exponent of the Formalist point of view among radical architects (Fig. 8). It is called a "communal residence" and dated 1919, but probably was in origin a pure experiment in form—in this case topped by castellated turret, a curious medievalism.

A real flowering of the visionary occurred internationally in the 1960s, and a number of important "schools" of visionaries of that decade are represented here: Archigram, the British comic-strip group, by Ron Herron (pp. 106, 107); the Austrians by Haus-Rucker-Co (pp. 116, 117); the Italian Superstudio (pp. 132, 133); Frederick Kiesler, the Austro-American (p. 116); and Paolo Soleri, Italo-American (pp. 110–13).

Sole representative of the current Postmodern movement in the United States is Roger C. Ferri, (pp. 108, 109) who, like so many of the current architectural reaction, is trying to reverse the mechanistic trend in urban design and make it more "townscapy" to the extent of draping greenery over the cliffs of skyscrapers.

5. UNUSUAL MATERIALS

Use of strange construction materials is an underlying theme of this book. To many it will indeed be phantastic to realize with what unconventional things structures can be built. Nearly one-quarter of the works were made with recycled materials of one sort or another—in many cases pure junk.

The individuals in this book have used their recycled materials in an individualistic, artistically creative, and often eccentric fashion, but it should be pointed out that not only do many dwellers in the *favelas*, i.e., squatter towns of third-world cities, use such stuff out of sheer necessity, but in recent years serious study has been given to the possibility that large-scale use of secondhand material could benefit low-cost housing programs.

A prime innovator in this movement has been the British architect Martin Pawley. He was consulted in 1972 by the Allende government of Chile—a country

which has had a long tradition of the poor self-constructing with scrounged materials, even license plates. In the following year Pawley supervised an intense study of recycled structure at the Cornell University School of Architecture. The result was a fascinating, and even phantastic, book entitled *Garbage Housing*, published by the Architectural Press of London in 1975. This book also deals extensively with the activities of Alfred Heineken, head of the old Dutch brewing company of that name, who, on visiting one of his major markets, the Dutch Caribbean island of Curaçao, took notice of (1) the shacks in which many people lived and (2) the litter of Heineken beer bottles. On his return home he had the Heineken bottle redesigned in a more rectangular shape called WOBO (WOrld BOttle), so that it could be used like a brick when emptied. The walls of such buildings give to the inside a luminous translucence much like the glass brick that was popular at one time in this country and the sidewalk insets that Luxfer Prism had made possible at the turn of the century.

Pawley makes clear that bottles have been used in the construction of load-bearing walls for a long time, cites worldwide examples in the nineteenth century, and illustrates a very snappy bottle-built motel in New Zealand and an exhibition center in Australia. The Chilean program experimented with a wide range of recycled materials. Pawley also illustrates a post-World War II governmental program in England to employ no longer needed sheet metal that had been manufactured for air raid shelters and military installations.

Designers here, however, seem to be interested in their secondhand materials for other than economic reasons, in fact, often simply for their picturesque effects. This is particularly true for those who employ bottles or other vitreous materials to achieve a built-in polychromy. George Plumb (pp. 138–41, 215), David Brown (pp. 144–47), Godfried Gabriel (pp. 152–55), and Grandma Prisbrey (pp. 156–59) used bottles structurally (Brown's similar to WOBOs), while Raymond Isidore (pp. 184, 185) employed broken glass to make a surface mosaic. Those who recycle masonry bits and ceramic scraps seem to be seeking similar coloristic effects: Ferdinand Cheval (pp. 66–69), Chief Rolling Thunder (p. 204), Howard Finster, who uses sculpted fragments (p. 236), and Juan O'Gorman, who used lava rock, itself actually having already been recycled by Nature (pp. 36, 37).

Scrap wood gives a rather more tattered appearance except for Kurt Schwitters' *Merzbau* (p. 43), perhaps because that was an in-house construction bursting up through several floors and out onto balconies, with which he and his family had to live. Mike Reynolds' (pp. 148–50) and Chomo's (pp. 206, 207) use of miscellaneous junk with which to build also looks rather scruffy, although more "aesthetic" treatment can be achieved of such random materials—witness Grandma Prisbrey and Sam Rodia (pp. 78–81). The tin-can house that Reynolds built for a lawyer in Taos, New Mexico, in 1973–74 was stuccoed over into very handsomely surfaced forms.

Use of scrap metal has a somewhat different cast—strongly Constructivist—as with Vic Moore (p. 205) or Pierre Avezard (pp. 220, 221), while Drop City (p. 208) is backyard Bucky Fuller (who gave Drop City his 1966 Dymaxion Award). Someone called Peter Rabbit said about Drop City in *Dome Book 2:*

Luke had all the panels ready to be put together when he arrived/he & Orville had cut the tops from junk cars with an axe/if you cut carefully around the edge you can get a 3½' X 7' sheet of 27 gauge steel with a baked on enamel surface from each car/3½' X 9' from station wagons/Droppers loved station wagons and panel trucks sent us into paroxysms of ecstasy.

Other unusual recycled materials become a bit surreal. Paper, for instance. Elis Stenman rolled newspapers, as many people do as a substitute for firewood, but then built his house of such rolls (p. 142), making it look as if he had built it with Lincoln Logs (which were, by the way, invented by one of the sons of Frank Lloyd Wright). Another "paper builder" is N. Molenaar, who made mosaics out of cigarbands (p. 176). But paper, like sheets of scrap metal, can also be used in technically advanced structures. In a book of 1974 called *Paper Houses* and dedicated to the way that paper or cardboard can be folded into geodesic (i.e., Bucky Fuller) panels to make domed, igloolike houses as at Drop City, there is illustrated one that was erected by the Charas Group in New York City (Fig. 11) in a study of low-cost or disaster housing. In case of disaster, such a geodesic dome is easy to build; all you have to do, as they say, is use "a 4 frequency triacon-type breakdown of the icosahedron...."!

Plastics can produce phantastic effects if draped: Chico (p. 143). Bones and skulls are also somewhat bizarre (p. 177). But strangest of all are buildings made of food products. In Mitchell, South Dakota, as part of a harvest festival every year since 1892, the local citizenry has resurfaced their Corn Palace with variously colored corn cobs, flax, oats, millet, proso, and cane, arranged as mosaic landscape, Indian encampment, the Sahara desert, what have you (Fig. 9). The present palace was erected in 1921, with Turkish domes for some reason added in the 1930s. Ten separate shades of corn—which we call Indian corn—are employed to produce colors in the mosaics. One is reminded of the wall of European corn (i.e., wheat) behind the table of celebrants in Pieter Brueghel's famous painting called *The Harvest Festival.*

9. *Corn Palace, Mitchell, South Dakota*

10. *Boboli Gardens, Florence, sixteenth century*

Much use of unusual materials is dedicated, as mentioned, to securing pictorial, polychromatic effects, whether it be shattered glass and ceramic with Isidore (pp. 184, 185), sea shells and other bits with Robert Vasseur (pp. 186–89) and Father Wernerus (p. 182), or Antonio Gaudí and his associates on the famous Park Güell mosaic benches in Barcelona (p. 126). There is indeed something homespun and friendly about the effect of structures so surfaced. For instance, a Gaudí fan recently visiting the Park Güell, wrote in a letter:

...in the Park Güell...how marvelous—the spontaneous response of children to the undulating, serpentine benches. My own daughter, Ariel, who is not quite seven, immediately began running. the length of them and in the process gained three small Spanish compatriots in her footsteps. No language was needed.

There remain a couple of other varieties of recycling, one of which is to readapt an *entire* existing structure for alternative use. This has been discussed above in connection with boats serving as housing. The Danish one in this section (p. 151) is unusual in that a boat in which persons *can* live is not employed in the usual boat-living ways, but more as a wooden tent. Another device is to recycle the earth itself so that it functions as walls and ceiling and not, as is customary, simply as a base, floor, or trench. Moles do this and so did Baldassare Forestiere in Fresno, California (pp. 160–63). Actually living underground in caves and tunnels that are natural or excavated, or around excavated court-patios—which in general is called troglodytic—is a worldwide phenomenon. There are in North Africa, Spain, and China well-known communities of excavated underground dwellings, and our own architects are beginning to go underground as a step toward conserving energy and saving surface acreage.

6. INTERIORS—EXTERIORS

An interesting aspect of the illustrations in this section, picturing as they do popular art tendencies rather than professional architectural decor, is that there are nearly twice as many examples in Europe as in the United States, whereas previous writers on the subject have made it out to be almost exclusively an American phenomenon. Jan Wampler, for instance, related the drive of the people whom he studied to the old New World custom of "building your own home," which these loners, largely born around the turn of the century, perpetuated whether native or immigrant. The Pompidou catalogue that has been mentioned attributes the artists' activity to ever-present marginal types on the American continent who buck the conventional "American Way of Life" and try to "realize themselves" by searching for new modes of action. The Walker Art Center's *Naïves and Visionaries* suggests that many of the American eccentric decorators of home and garden have been possessed with "obsessive social and religious views."

As no two works in this section are alike in either style or iconographic message, and as it is hard to find similarity in any but a few, they have been arranged here purely pictorially to be savored for their phantastic appearance, however rational the creators may have considered themselves to be. Many of those whom I have cited as being similar in some sense are so purely by coincidence, as they are on different continents and could hardly have seen each other's works.

So there is apparently no North American monopoly on phantastic architecture. In fact, it pops up anywhere and most everywhere in the Western world. This one (Fig. 12), however, popped up in Japan in Hayajima town (Okayama prefecture), some 350 miles south of Tokyo. It is a coffee shop along National Highway 2. Popped up? Or dropped down? As it is architecturally in Western, not Japanese, style, it probably was built in some Western land. The exact opposite point to this part of Japan on the globe of the Earth is in the Atlantic Ocean well off Montevideo, Uruguay, but as the house is slightly tilted, it probably came through the Earth from the direction of its tilt, that is, somewhere around Montevideo itself. This is real sci fi!

This section of the book's pictures is, in fact, full of phantastic illusions. Street art makes you believe that something is where it is not (pp. 190, 191), with a cat (not shown) in the window of one and a fellow in the bathtub in the other. There is a variety of such illusions in interiors (pp. 192–95) and there are building exteriors that appear to be groves of trees (p. 175), or a rocky shore with seaweed (p. 127), or even Hell itself (p. 174).

These, like the upside-down Uruguayan coffeehouse in Japan, are publicly understood illusions. This is to say that their fictions are readily understood visually, being representative of situations of general acquaintanceship or understanding. But a number of buildings here—mainly residences—are decorated on the inside or outside, or both, with painting, sculpture, or mosaic that is perfectly clear in its forms, but totally obscure in meaning because it represents highly subjective and often personally mystic formulations. This includes Junker in Germany (pp. 165–69); Monsieur G. (pp. 172, 173), Dhièvre (pp. 179–81), Isidore (pp. 184, 185), and Chomo (pp. 206, 207) in France; and St. Eom in the United States (p. 178).

And then there are those punsters everywhere who choose to treat the front of a building, the facade, as if it were indeed the face of man or beast or devil, among them the Saint Phalle team (p. 52), Salvador Dali (p. 41), Bruno Weber (p. 46), Rudolf Steiner's first Goetheanum (p. 129), the Parisian nightclub (p. 174), and the Bomarzo garden (p. 216).

7. GARDENS

The design of a garden, while not strictly speaking architecture, actually represents in clearest, often sculptural, form the aspirations of the phantasts to whom this volume is dedicated.

Gardens are, actually, more closely related to city planning in that from the seventeenth century on, when the great gardens of France were being laid out at the country seats of monarchs, cardinals, ministers, and aristocrats, the early designers of them, André Le Nôtre for example, experimented with formal layouts that were subsequently applied to public spaces and public parks in cities such as Paris. When in the eighteenth century landscaping went irregular and picturesque, bits of that sort were added to formal gardens, as at Caserta in Italy, and picturesque landscaping for a long time affected new city-street layouts, especially under the influence of the informal landscape architects in Britain.

What are essentially gardens have also been used as town or city substitutes—witness Disneyland, California, and Disneyworld, Florida. A somewhat more sober garden-town (not to be confused with British Garden City theory, which is a town invaded by a garden) is that of Portmeirion, Northern Wales. It is a twenty-acre village composed of buildings of different purposes and in a variety of styles, all executed by the architect-owner of the property, Sir Clough Williams-Ellis, during the 1920s and 1930s in order to fulfill his childhood dream of erecting an ensemble of buildings conforming to his own ideas of fitness, wit, and contextual planning. If Sir Clough had lived in the eighteenth century, it would have been called a "folly."

Some of the examples in this garden section do have architectural implications, albeit miniature and phantastic ones: Marcel Landreau in France (p. 236) and Howard Finster (p. 236) in the United States. Architectural follies, which are generally referred to as foolish, extravagant, and useless, were not necessarily so when the actual reasons for their execution are explored. Although even the ancients had follies in their backyards, the term is especially reserved for aberrations of the

11. *Charas, ¾ sphere geodesic dome of paper panels*

12. *Coffee shop in Japan*

13. *Mermaid Fountain, Bingham Park, Craigmillar, Edinburgh*

wealthy during the Romantic period of the late eighteenth and early nineteenth centuries. The Chevalier de Monville, who perversely designed his estate in the form of a desert of devastation, had built there a residence in the form of a gigantic, ruined, classical column (pp. 84, 85) and an icebox/tomb (essentially the same function) in the form of a pyramid (p. 243)—important symbol of the geometrical, classical, and the everlasting for philosophers and artists of that period known as Romantic Classicism. Equally serious was the arch that had been erected on the estate of British Admiral Anson, which was in a sense a scholarly publication. In 1751, a pair of British architects, James Stuart and Nicholas Revett, traveled to Athens under the sponsorship of the British Society of Dilettanti and spent three years there making what were probably the first really accurate measurements of the major Greek and Roman monuments in that ancient city—then occupied by the Turks and not often seen. Their publication of several volumes of *The Antiquities of Athens* after their return (1762, 1787, and 1794, the last two after Stuart's death) was fundamental to the Classical Revival, in particular Volume II in which their drawings of the Parthenon made clear that the Greek Doric Order was basically quite different from the Roman (illustrated in their first volume), thereby totally transforming the whole aesthetic of the Classical Revival. Actually, this information had been available long before the delayed publication of Volume II because James (called "Athenian") Stuart was engaged as an architect to erect small replicas of several Athenian buildings in a number of British estate gardens. He did several for Admiral Anson, including this one in 1761 (p. 244), a reproduction of the Emperor Hadrian's Arch which they had measured but which was not pictured until publication of Volume III a third of a century later. So its erection was of much more historic consequence than celebrating the voyage around the world of Admiral Anson (who died in 1762); it was essentially a learned monograph standing in the garden.

Less serious, perhaps, were the two tall towers constructed about 1800 for George Messiter (p. 243) and "Mad" Jack Fuller (p. 245), although the former *was* used to provide employment during a temporary slump of the local textile industry. Also less weighty are the two recent follies by Van Praag, a Neo-Classicist (p. 243), and Avezard, an apparent Dadaist (pp. 220, 221).

The folkish garden designs are more involved with sculptural figures, in some cases quite iconic and arresting in character (pp. 222–33 passim.). Some can be said to be quite earnest, as Camille Vidal and his Noah's Ark (p. 226), or Adolphe-Julien Fouéré, who seems to have been quite vengeful in his art about local brigands (pp.

234, 235). All the others appear to be engaged in pure phantasy even if, as has been suggested, certain ones were motivated by deep religious beliefs.

The sixteenth-century Bomarzo park near Viterbo, Italy, is a prototype for the sculpture/architecture mix of many of these gardens. Another forerunner of them are the Boboli Gardens at the Palazzo Pitti in Florence, the most phantastic portion of which is the grotto—a type of artificial cave that has already been discussed in connection with castles. Designed by the architect Bernardo Buontalenti and his followers, it is an amazing combination of architectural entrance, artificial stalactitic caves, illusionistic wall paintings in fresco, and shaggy human and animal sculptures including, tucked in, four of Michelangelo's famous *Slaves* (Fig. 10) that he had begun to carve for the 1520s version of the Tomb of Pope Julius II. (His originals have been removed from the Boboli grotto to a museum in Florence.)

Other major elements that are designed for gardens are fixtures such as walls, benches, and various pieces of furniture. The latter usually are of a "rustic" style that has at times come to influence house furniture. More substantial are the heavy walls and benches, often undulating as has been noted, in Gaudí's Park Güell (p. 126) and St. Eom's yard (p. 178), made of solid coral rock by Edward Leedskalnin (p. 237), or of concrete with bits of color embedded in it, as by Herman Rusch (p. 242). One of the latest of such park furnishings is a fountain in the form of a reclining mermaid (with water jets in her mouth and tail), made of concrete reinforced with mesh wire in a shape over which children can climb and slide (Fig. 13). In Bingham Park of Craigmillar, a part of Edinburgh, Scotland, it was constructed with community aid during the summer of 1979. It was commissioned by the Craigmillar Festival Society, supervised by three professionals led by the sculptor Pedro Silva of New York City, and was carried out by local teenagers and adults in order to "upgrade and visually improve the local environment." Colorful mosaics of broken tile will cover it, much as the Gaudí benches, but after the design of local residents as at General Grant's Tomb in New York.

As regards the trimming of growth and the artificial shaping of vegetation in a garden, this art of topiary seems from most ancient times to have been one of phantasy. It is a controversial art. Joseph Addison, the eighteenth-century English essayist and statesman, commented: "I would rather look upon a tree in all its luxuriancy and diffusion of boughs and branches, than when thus cut and trimmed into a mathematical figure." We have a wide range of topiary depicted here (pp. 211, 238–41). The other "natural" art of the garden is that of

flowers and flower beds which have in the last centuries so largely supplanted the earlier concentration on herb growing. Flowers wither, of course, and are seasonal in most climes, but not for Romano Gabriel (pp. 212, 213) and George Plumb (p. 215) whose "gardens" bloom permanently because they are made of wood and bottles, respectively.

Which brings us back to where we started. What is fantasy (phantasy) anyway?

George R. Collins

THE ARTISTS

One of Robert Tatin's dragons

EDWARD JAMES

Right and overleaf: Edward James was born into a wealthy family in Scotland in 1907. He worked for a time in the diplomatic service, wrote poetry, and made friends with artists such as Tchelitchew, Dali, and Magritte. He formed an important collection of Surrealist art that is housed at the Edward James Foundation in England.

For the past twenty-five years James has lived in Xilitla, Mexico, where he started building, with the help of the villagers, a series of fantastic palaces, temples, pagodas, and fountains populated with a variety of animals—tigers, flamingos, crocodiles, deer, boa constrictors, and other birds. His dream is to stay in one of

his houses called The House Shaped Like a Whale, in which the animals would sleep near his bed.

James, who has never studied architecture, combines many different styles in his buildings, from Greek to Gothic to Romanesque. Some of the elements he painted in very bright colors and he named some of them Summer Palace with Orange Windows, Red Temple by the Waterfall, Homage to Max Ernst, and Balinese Baldachins. Walking through James' jungle, one has the feeling of discovering a lost city because over the years the luxuriant undergrowth has covered many of his creations, making them even stranger.

GIOVANNI BATTISTA PIRANESI

The renowned artist Piranesi, born near Venice, Italy, in 1720, studied architecture and etching in Venice and Rome. By the time he was twenty-three years old he had already published his first large volume of etchings on architecture. Settling permanently in Rome in 1745, he devoted the rest of his life to evoking the grandeur of the Eternal City in prints. His dramatic, very personal Views

of Rome are extremely popular, but they are not an exact rendering of the ancient and baroque monuments, but his own poetic, artistic rearrangement. Here he has jumbled together existing and imagined funerary monuments, urns, and busts into this towering Vision of the Via Appia, an etching that introduces his volume Le antichità romane.

Stairs in the House with the Three, Maybe Five Floors.

Temple by the waterfall for the ducks.

House for the parrots.

Place San Eduardo with Edward James near the fountain.

House destined to be a cinema.

Homage to Max Ernst.

Summer palace with James standing in the middle.

Entrance and stairs to the future cinema.

JUAN O'GORMAN

The Mexican architect and artist Juan O'Gorman, known for his design for the university library in Mexico City, built his house from 1956 to 1961 on a volcanic rock formation in the Pedregal of San Angel in Mexico City. A grotto in the lava rock provided the living room and the rest of the house was built in strange shapes of the same lava rock. The interior and exterior of the house were covered with mosaics representing jaguars, condors, Mayan serpents, Aztec warriors, and abstract symbols from the ancient Indian cultures of Latin America.

O'Gorman's work, like much contemporary Mexican art, showed a retention of some good lessons from the past with a melding of architecture, sculpture, and decoration.

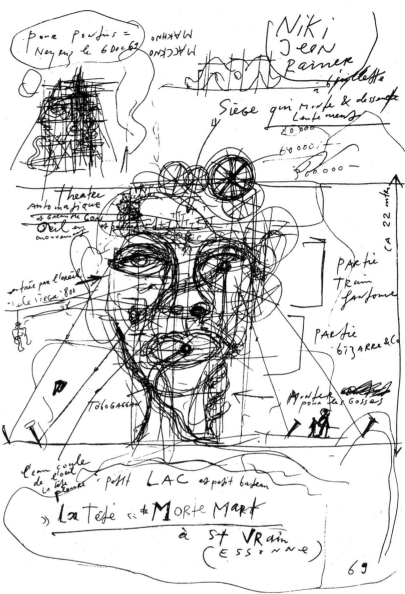

LE MONSTRE DANS LA FORÊT

A structure in the form of a gigantic, disembodied head. Under construction since 1970, this Monster in the Forest is a collaborative project that involves a team of artists including Bernhard Luginbühl, Niki de Saint Phalle, Eva Aeppli, Daniel Spoerri, Foknoz and others. Inside the head, some 80 feet high, are lofts where artists can create a kind of fun fair featuring theatrical and improvisational art. This "super-collaboration-individual-long-distance-permanent-collective Gigantoleums-apparat" will be open to delight visitors. But the participating artists also relish the thought that in the distant future the abandoned head will be rediscovered—an amusing artifact of the culture that created it.

SALVADOR DALI

One of the most illustrious and most outrageous of the Surrealist painters, Dali (born 1904) can be expected to do the unexpected.
Left: The Salvador Dali Museum in his birthplace of Figueras, Spain, has this walk-in Face of Mae West.

Right: Much of Dali's imagery focuses on psychotic obsessions, hallucinations, and remembrances. His design for the Amsterdam Airport shopping center (1976) is haunting and not for the weak.

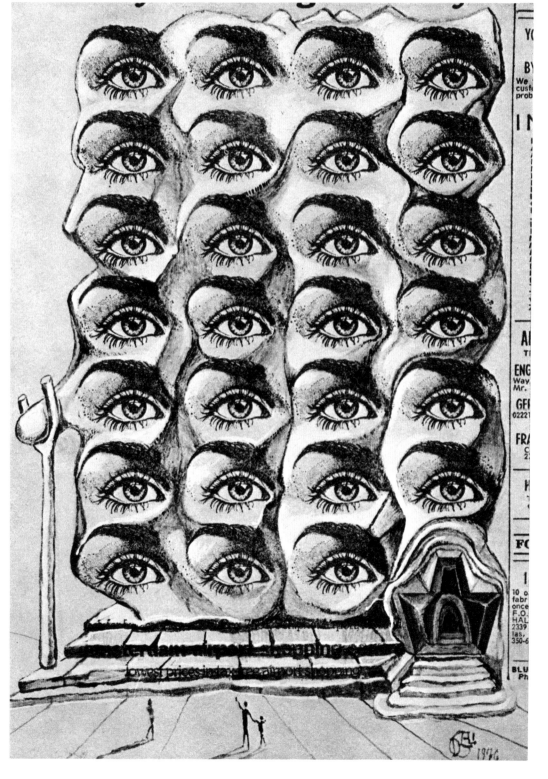

JEAN DUBUFFET, CLOSERIE FALBALLA

Top: At his four-acre estate in Perigny-sur-Yerres, a small village near Paris, Jean Dubuffet in 1970 began his most ambitious sculptural/architectural project, the Closerie Falballa. Constructed of polystyrene and concrete, these "cloisters" consist of a large amorphous structure called the Villa Falballa, the surrounding sculptured gardens, and the undulating walls that partially enclose the ensemble. Inside the Villa is an inner sanctum known as the Cabinet Logologique containing twenty-two wall panels teeming with the cellular white forms and doodlelike

sinuous lines that have made Dubuffet's works so famous.

Surrounding the Villa is an elaborately terraced garden, landscaped with interlocking jigsaw-patterned slabs. Black, pin-striped lines meander across the pure white ground. Here, as in all his works executed between 1962 and 1974 (known as the Hourloupe *series), Dubuffet creates an environment where ambiguity reigns supreme, where natural forms and abstract figuration, the objective world and our subjective perceptions are free to commingle playfully.*

KURT SCHWITTERS, MERZBAU

Right: Kurt Schwitters, born in Hanover in 1887, was one of the members of the Dada group of artists who revolted against traditional values in art. He coined the word Merz *from the German word* Kommerz *and used it for any of his works that employed old rubbish and other found objects. The Merzbau (Merz structure), both the*

architectural elements and the interior, dates from the 1920s when Schwitters began to turn his junk collections and house in Hanover into this wonderful building. Here is a perfect example of the Dada ideal of abolishing the distinction between art and life. The structure was destroyed during the bombings of Hanover in 1943.

ROBERT TATIN, LA FRÊNOUSE

Robert Tatin was born in 1902 in Mayenne, France. His art was influenced by his childhood surroundings—oat and cabbage fields—but he seems not to have had any formal art training. Later, living in the nearby town of Laval, Tatin tried a number of different jobs—tailor, pastry cook, mason, and general laborer. He also worked from time to time as a coal dealer, house painter, and cabinetmaker. After World War II, he began to make ceramic buttons and brooches, which became very much in vogue. His witty crockery made him successful. In 1951, Tatin and his wife went to Brazil, where his work was shown in the Bienal *of São Paulo. They returned in 1962 to the region where he was born, and Tatin bought an old farm, La Frênouse, in Cossé-Le-Vivien. He restored it completely and built his house of figurative architecture, with the Giant Gate, Moon and Sun Gates, the Dragon, Adam and Eve—a whole universe of archaic reminiscences made of cement and ceramics. It is now a museum where Tatin teaches ceramics and painting.*

Weber in his studio.

Living room with fertility figure.

Chairs for the visitors.

Snake bridge.

One of the dream monsters.

Front view of the house.

BRUNO WEBER

Top, left, and overleaf: Bruno Weber was born in 1931 in Dietikon, near Zurich, Switzerland. Seventeen years ago he began to construct his studio and paradise garden on the plot of ground belonging to his parents, who were farmers in Dietikon. Weber lives there from the proceeds of the sale of his paintings, etchings, and chairs in plastic.

His work conjures up images of strange oriental cultures and fairy tales with mythological figures. The living room has four symbols: water, fire, air, and fertility. The woman—fertility—has two small doors in her middle through which food is hauled from the kitchen below.

Opposite: Detail of the entrance.

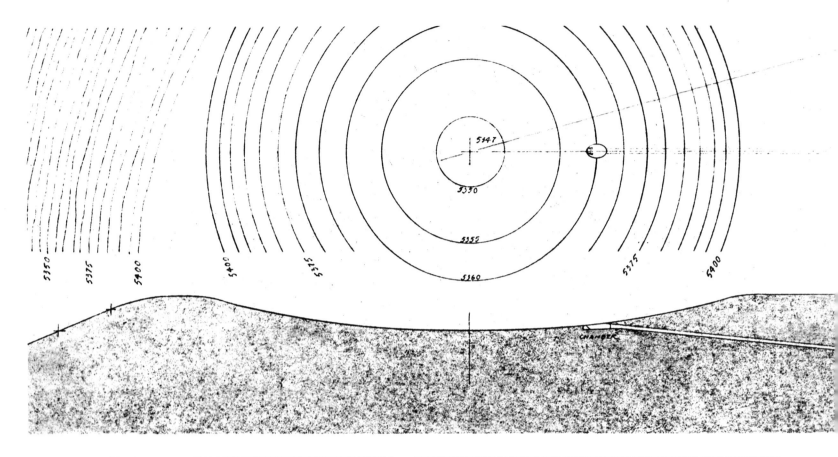

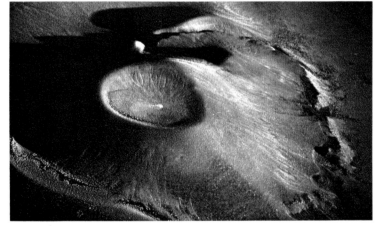

JIM TURRELL, RODEN CRATER PROJECT

Set in the stark beauty of the Painted Desert in Arizona, the Roden Crater Project is a bold experiment in perceptual art that draws its power from the very elements of nature. One of a handful of West Coast artists who in the mid-1960s began to use light as a medium, Jim Turrell became captivated by the optical effects he observed while flying his private aircraft over the desert. Turrell began searching for an environment in the desert that could become a kind of peephole into the kaleidoscopic interplay of earth, light, and space. Thus began the Roden Crater Project, which is still under construction.

One begins at the house located outside the rim of the volcanic crater. Apertures in the structure create "light sculptures" in the chamber and other optical effects, while the elevated walkway outside provides an observation point to view the subtle changes in light and space that play across the desert. To enter the crater one walks through a one-fourth-mile-long tunnel that gently ascends so that the rim of the crater is always visible at the end of the tunnel. Emerging from the tunnel, one is struck by how the sky seems to have been transformed into a celestial vault.

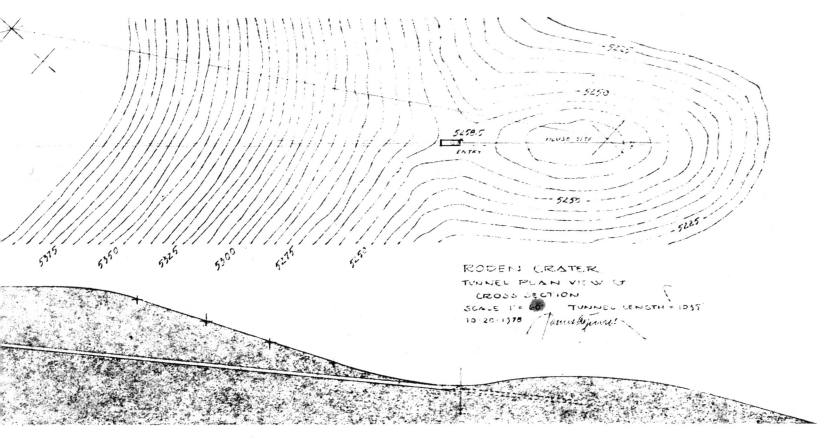

RODEN CRATER
TUNNEL PLAN VIEW &
CROSS SECTION
SCALE 1" = 60'   TUNNEL LENGTH = 1055'
10·20·1978

NIKI DE SAINT PHALLE

Niki de Saint Phalle, born in Neuilly, France, in 1930, was part of a group of artists called the Nouveaux Réalistes (New Realists), which was formed in 1960. Her polyester "Nanas" (large female figures), begun as simple sculptures done in vivid colors, have grown larger and larger with time and finally became so large that they could be entered. Her sculpture/architecture is baroque, joyous, and playful. The materials used are papier-mâché, concrete, paint, or concrete and polyester.

This house for Roger Nellens, a Belgian industrialist (in Knokke, Belgium), was begun in 1972. Nellens requested a large sculpture in the garden, which could serve as house and playground. Referring to all of these giant fantasy figures, Niki de Saint Phalle said: "I am the Nana dream house; inside of me you can put anything you wish: a bar, a bed, a library, a chapel. I am an adult doll house...a refuge for dreaming."

This all came about because when Niki was 25 years old she saw the Palais Idéal of the postman Cheval and buildings by Gaudí. "They changed my life."

She *is the gigantic, inhabitable "sculpture" done in 1966 for the Modern Museum of Stockholm. Collaborating with Jean Tinguely and the Swedish Per Olof Ultvedt, Niki de Saint Phalle built this funny, female giant of chicken wire, fabric, and glue. Like all her giant sculptures,* She *was painted in gay, bright colors. Red and green lights controlled traffic at the entrance. Once inside, one could visit the bar in one breast, toboggan down a thigh, exit through the navel and enjoy the view, watch a Greta Garbo film, and listen to music and clanking mechanical sculptures.*

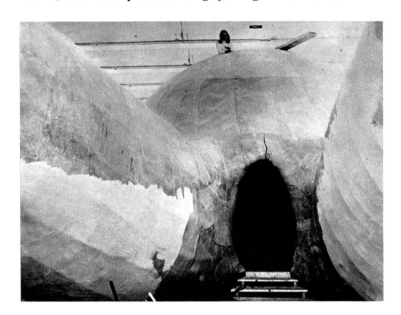

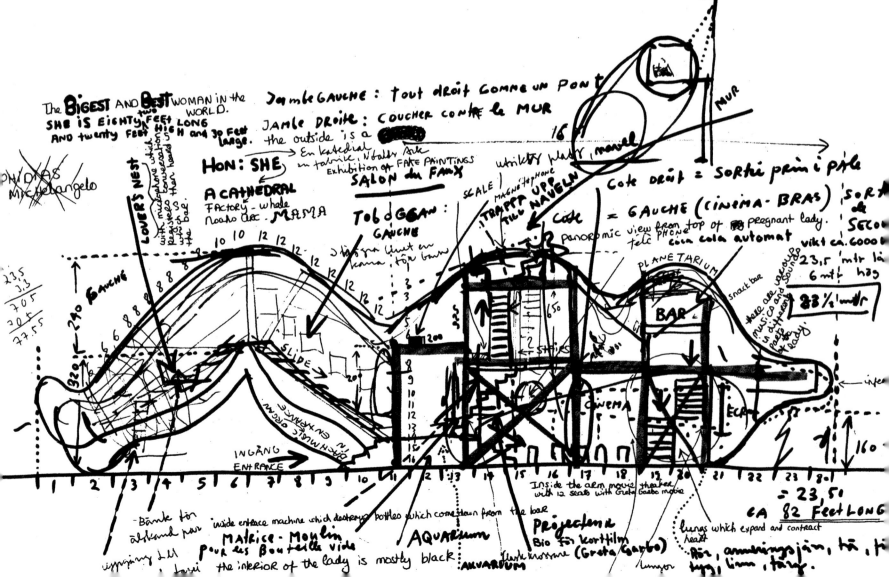

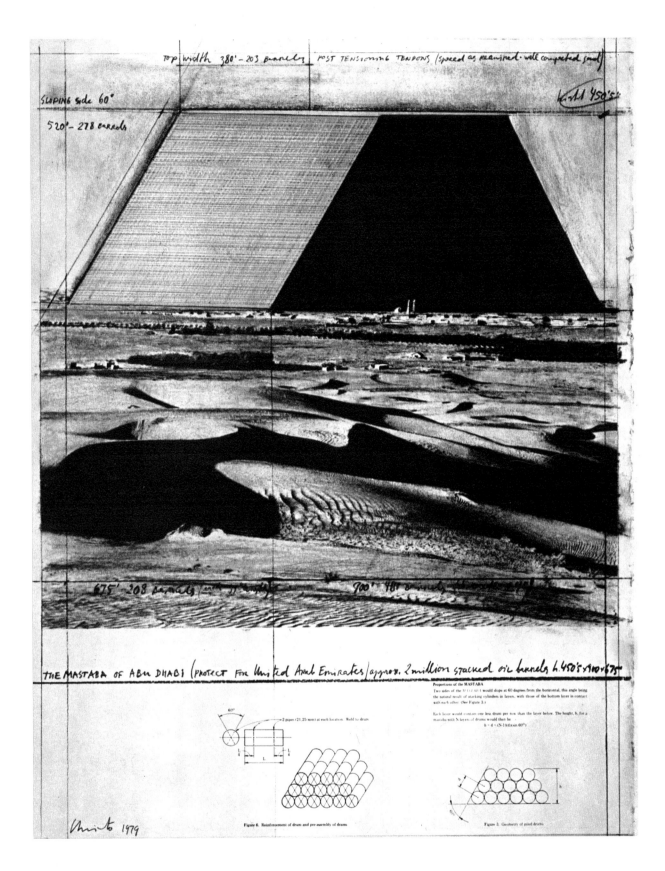

CHRISTO, MASTABA OF ABU DHABI

Known for his wrapped coastline and buildings, Valley Curtain, *and* Running Fence, *the artist Christo is plan-* *ning to stack two million oil barrels in this project for the United Arab Emirates.*

CASTLES AND TOWERS

Pieter Wiersma's sand castle

KING LUDWIG II, GROTTO OF VENUS

Left: An artificial grotto, the Grotto of Venus was designed in 1875 by Fidelis Schabet and built in the following year for King Ludwig II of Bavaria. Called the "Mad King," Ludwig constructed palace after palace—Neuschwanstein, Herrenchiemsee, and Linderhof, where this grotto can be found. It was inspired by Capri's Blue Grotto and the Venus Grotto in Richard Wagner's opera Tannhäuser. *Thirty-three feet high and several hundred feet long, it appears to be rock, but is really brick and iron covered with canvas and cement. The grotto contains an illuminated lake, swans, a golden shell-shaped boat in which Ludwig was rowed by a servant, and a huge painting of a scene from* Tannhäuser.

PRINCE OF PALAGONIA, VILLA PALAGONIA

Overleaf: In the eighteenth century, in Bagheria near Palermo, Sicily, the Prince of Palagonia, a hunchback, conceived and had built a palace of monsters as deformed as himself. Among his dreams in stone was the walkway with an ornate balustrade of sculptures: monsters with five or six heads, donkeys standing like men, lions at the table with napkins under their chins and gobbling oysters, and ostriches carrying baskets. At the entrance to the villa are a dwarf on a dolphin with the head of a Roman emperor, and an emperor with two noses and a crown of thorns. Ironically, the prince fathered a son who proved to be a beautiful child.

A LEBANESE CASTLE

Above and right: In the neighborhood of Beit et Dine, a Lebanese built a castle decorated with sculptures, reliefs, and a flaming inscription "Lebanon Forever."

ISTVÁN TARÓDI

Left: In 1959, former housepainter István Taródi bought land outside Sopron, Hungary, near the Austrian border. A year later, in the time free from his work in a textile factory, he started to build this "medieval" castle. By 1977, three towers of the castle were completed and Taródi now lives there with his wife. He thinks he will be finished with two more towers of his "irregular fortress" by about 1985.

PIETER WIERSMA, SAND CASTLES

Pieter Wiersma works as an architect for Monumenten-
zorg (Monument Maintenance) in Holland. On weekends,
he gives expression to his love for Gothic architecture by
building sand castles, fortresses, and cathedrals on the
Dutch North Sea beaches. By now he has built about sev-
enty of them. His sand castles' architecture often comes
from his imagination; occasionally he copies a real castle.
Wiersma starts to build early in the morning. Shortly
before sunset he is finished and carefully records his work
in photographs—the only things that remain since the
castles are washed away. The absence of people in the pho-
tographs results in an almost surrealistic lack of scale.

JOSEPH FERDINAND CHEVAL, IDEAL PALACE

Top, right, and overleaf: Joseph Ferdinand Cheval was born in 1836 not far from Hauterives in the French Drôme. At the age of 31 he became a postman. In 1879, in Hauterives, he began to build his Palais Idéal (Ideal Palace), which was realized in two stages. For the next thirty-three years he built this monument and tomb to himself with stones, mosaic chips, glass fragments, and his own kind of reinforced concrete. He taught himself masonry and made these strange stone creatures, animals, and plants.

In 1912, the palace was completed and Cheval began to prepare himself for old age. However, he discovered that according to French law he must be buried in a public cemetery. So he built a second tomb in the public cemetery, which was completed in 1922. Cheval died in 1924, at the age of 88.

Cheval was the idol of the Surrealists, and his palace subsequently became a tourist attraction. Both the palace and the tomb have been placed on the list of national monuments.

Top: Detail of his tomb.

Right: Overall view of the Palais Idéal with Cheval and his wife.

ROBERT GARCET, TOWER OF THE APOCALYPSE

Left and below: Born in 1912, Robert Garcet is a stonecutter by profession. Around 1930, he settled in Fort Eben-Emael, Belgium, building a house there, then a workshop. In the early fifties, he began the Tour de l'Apocalypse. Garcet sees the church as the cause of today's chaos. He pleads for the reinterpretation of the Bible and the study of the past in order to obtain knowledge for the future. Garcet is considered an eccentric and has met with much hostility. Ever since the tower was completed in 1964, Garcet has lived there most of the time.

Wall reliefs in the cellar.

Column with the four symbols of the Apocalypse.

ED GALLOWAY, MONUMENT TO THE AMERICAN INDIAN

Right and far right: This Monument to the American Indian was made of concrete towers and buildings which were embellished with Indian symbols and motifs. Ed Galloway built the monument from 1936 to 1948, after he retired to Sandsprings, Oklahoma.

ICE CASTLES AND SCULPTURES

Ice can be as hard as bricks and cement—in cold weather.
Left: A great snow castle in Davos, Switzerland.

Top: This dazzling Ice Palace was created by students of
the Fine Arts School in Quebec, Canada. It is lit up at
night. Anyone without the proper carnival spirit is sen-
tenced to a stay in the icy dungeon.

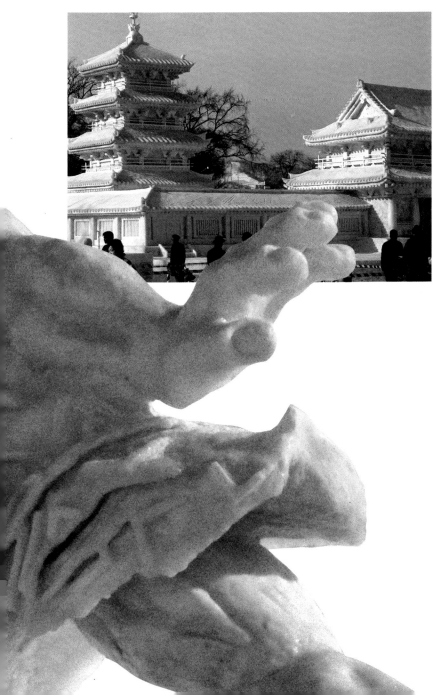

SIMON RODIA,
WATTS TOWERS

Here and overleaf: Born in Naples between 1875 and 1880, Simon Rodia (originally Simone Rodilla) came to America when he was ten years old. Later Rodia earned his living as a night guard, construction worker, and layer of tiles. It was around 1921 that he began to work on the Watts Towers on a triangular piece of land that he had bought in the Los Angeles suburb of Watts. He bent steel rods, covering them with cement inlaid with mosaic tile, small pieces of glass and pottery, shells, and sometimes whole bottles. The cement and steel he bought; the rest of the materials were discards.

His motivation is unknown. He did want to build "something great." The tallest of his three towers is in excess of 102 feet. The neighbors could not understand the eccentric builder and became hostile toward him, while Rodia became more and more isolated. When recently questioned by a photographer, his neighbors had different reactions to the towers. One of them used the towers as a landmark to get home when he was drunk. Another called the FBI during World War II, thinking there was a spy ring. The third man said he had never seen the towers.

In 1954, when Rodia was about 79, he sold or deeded his property and everything on it to a neighbor and moved to the San Francisco area. In the late fifties the towers made news. The city of Los Angeles wanted to demolish them, but a committee of interested parties was formed to fight the city. A test was given to determine whether the towers satisfied building requirements, and they did. Rodia lived to see films and books dedicated to his towers, but he died before the towers were placed on the list of national monuments.

BUILDINGS AS...

A snail-shell outhouse in Boulogne-la-Grasse, France

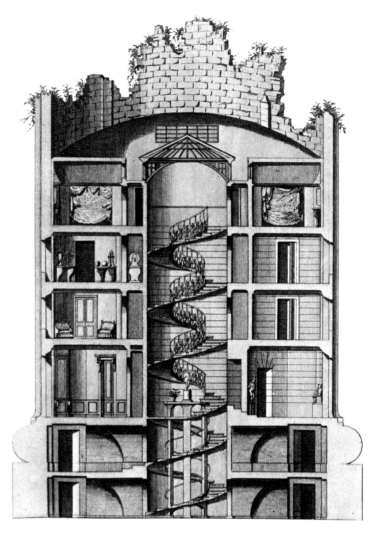

Chevalier Racine de Monville, a rich dandy, had this column house built around 1780 after a design by the architect François Barbier. Constructed on his estate and park called the Desert of Retz, near Marly, it was in the shape of a Doric column fallen into ruins. De Monville actually lived and entertained lavishly in this house.

Vue Perspective de la Colonne.

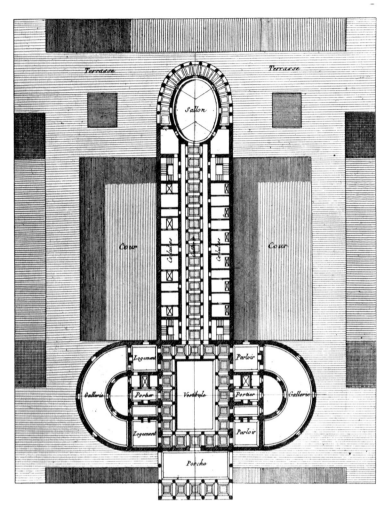

This house of pleasure, laid out like a phallus, was designed by Claude-Nicolas Ledoux in the eighteenth century, but it was never executed.

Here is a design by the eighteenth-century French architect Jean-Jacques Lequeu for a "cow barn on a cool meadow," as he wrote. The space in the cow's body was a storehouse for straw, grain, oats, and hay, and the eyes were for light and air. On either side were stone troughs for water.

Fig. 174.

les Peches ... Lapiece aclire
Au dessus, le genies à geulles de metal, dardie
et du fein four four et la lerne reçoit la lumiere des yeux se la sere ...
que servent de laire a la charpente d'ar.

...chei tournée au midi, est sur la fraicheprairie.

A gras yatin
clochette d'argent à des bords de
gaderand
couverte d'une housse de Cachemire
ouvree et brossée d'or et d'argent q...

87

A fantasy in the eighteenth century, buildings in the shape of animals and things were actually constructed in the twentieth century—many of them and all over the world.

Left: The Old Lady's Shoe is in Nehru Park in Bombay, India.

Below: The nursery rhyme "The Little Old Lady Who Lived in a Shoe" was taken literally by the Claytons on the island of Jersey, England. They really entertain so many children they don't know what to do. Originally, the shoe came from a children's playground, but it fulfilled Danny Clayton's childhood ambition to make his first home in a shoe.

Right: Sometimes the objects depicted are relevant to the type of establishment or to the place, such as the cowboy boots in Texas, which serve as restrooms.

Riesenfaß-Baude Bad Liebwerda.

Far left: Hot-dog food stand.

Top: A barrel house in Bad Liebwerda, Isergebirge, Czechoslovakia.

Left: Closed and seemingly uninhabited, Poseidon's Horse, as this house is known, continues to stare at the sea in Gargaliani, southern Greece.

Right: James V. Lafferty patented a design for an elephant house in 1882, and in the following year this pachyderm was constructed near Atlantic City, New Jersey.

Below: Michael's Restaurant in Florida invites guests into a covered wagon.

Far right: A sombrero Texaco station.

Right, bottom: Why a tractor for an office building in California?

Right and far right: In 1761, the Earl of Dunmore had a two-story-high pineapple house built on the grounds of Dunmore Castle (Stirlingshire, Scotland), which was to serve as his country residence. The eccentric earl later became governor of Virginia, then of New York. With all its spiky leaves, the 40-foot-high pineapple has remained in existence to this day and an ingenious drainage system has helped it withstand the elements. In Scotland's grey and northern climate, this tropical fruit continues to flourish.

Below: In Storyland, a 50-acre park with stories and verses in Neptune, New Jersey, kids can visit this birthday-cake house and celebrate their birthdays in grand style.

Below right: A children's mushroom house in Efteling Park, Kaatsheuvel, Holland.

STOP

1. CAR IN NEUTRAL

2. FOOT OFF BRAKE

3. HANDS OFF WHEEL

To have your car washed in a whale makes sense, Jonah!

Below: An old casino designed like a boat in Enghien-les-Bains, Val d'Oise, France.

Far below: This house, as a boat, in California gives a feeling of solidity, homeyness, and the thrill of the sea—without seasickness.

Right: A house shaped like an ocean liner is in Boulogne, France, and was designed by Georges-Henri Pingusson, a pupil of the architect Le Corbusier.

Far right: In Martinique, a villa in the form of a boat looks as if ready to be launched.

THE VISIONARIES

Wassili Luckhardt, Monument to Labor, *1919–20*

VISIONARY SPHERICAL HOUSES

Claude-Nicolas Ledoux, Étienne-Louis Boullée, and Jean-Jacques Lequeu were well-known French architects of the eighteenth and early nineteenth century. While some of their concepts were realized, much of their present-day *fame comes from their visionary drawings and designs. These were often based on simple geometric forms (the sphere being the most perfect), smooth surfaces, and bold scale—all resulting in a highly symbolic architecture.*

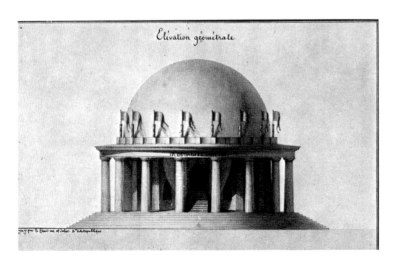
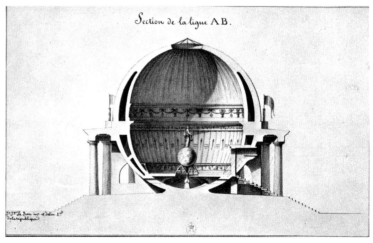

Opposite page, top: Étienne-Louis Boullée, four views of a projected monument to Isaac Newton, 1784.

Opposite page, bottom: Jean-Jacques Lequeu, project for a Temple of Equality.

Top this page: Claude-Nicolas Ledoux, project for a cooper's workshop, 1773–79.

Bottom this page: Claude-Nicolas Ledoux, project for a rural caretaker's house, c. 1780.

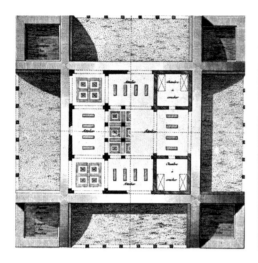

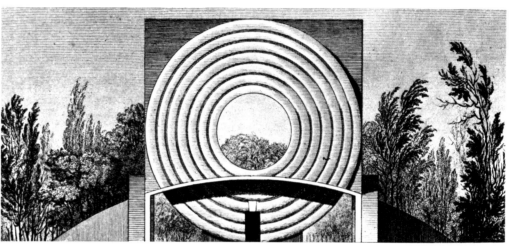

BUCKMINSTER FULLER, FLOATING GEODESIC SPHERES

Above: These enormous space stations depicted floating eerily over mountain peaks would seem to be from the world of science-fiction fantasy. But these Floating Geodesic Spheres are viable aircraft that could be realized with today's technology, according to their designer R. Buckminster Fuller, the renowned inventor, architect, author, and philosopher. Although resembling a space-age craft, these spheres, patented by Fuller in 1967, actually would function on the same aerodynamic principle as the hot-air balloon of yesteryear. Called tensegrity (tensional integrity) spheres, the structure is to be built of aluminum spars strung together in triangular and hexagonal space-frame units to form a sphere measuring a half mile in diameter. Over this rigid skeleton would be stretched a double-layer plastic skin that would act as a kind of one-way solar mirror.

As the sun's rays pass into the sphere, the air inside becomes slightly warmer, and the expanding air escapes through one-way valves. Thus, the air trapped inside the sphere becomes lighter than the surrounding atmosphere, exerting a buoyant upward pressure on the craft. With such spheres Fuller foresees creating floating tetrahedronal cities, air-deliverable skyscrapers, flyable dwelling machines—and much more!

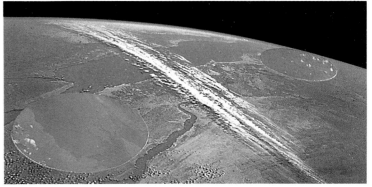

THOMAS SHANNON, AIRBORNE ISLANDS

Above and far right: In his Airborne Island series created between 1973 and 1979, New York artist Thomas Shannon gives us a visionary version of the proverbial "cloud nine." His Airborne Islands are garden parks which literally float like a cloud from one area to another. A shallow, circular valley two miles in diameter is covered by a mile-high transparent membrane dome that permits the sun's rays to drench the lush landscape and heat the balmy atmosphere inside. Hovering a mile above the earth and reached by air ferries, these integrated ecosystems offer a refreshing retreat from the uncomfortable climate below, stimulating educational and cultural facilities, and an idyllic environment for recreation and relaxation.

RON HERRON, WALKING CITIES, NO. 27

This orthographic rendering of a visionary megastructure, executed in 1964, is typical of the work of Ron Herron, who has been associated with the British Archigram group since 1961. This mobile urban module is conceived to be one of an indefinite number of such autonomous units which together form a Walking City. In the futuristic world envisioned by Herron, these complexes would meander across the landscape like gigantic bugs, forming aggregates with other megastructures and uncoupling after a while to seek new configurations. At first glance the Walking City seems to be based on a seemingly absurd contradiction: the megastructures embody the highest level of technology and social organization, while their aggregate, the Walking City, resembles an insect colony. But the contradiction is deliberate and characteristic of the Archigram concept of modern society as mobile, dynamic, and ever discarding the obsolete to embrace innovation.

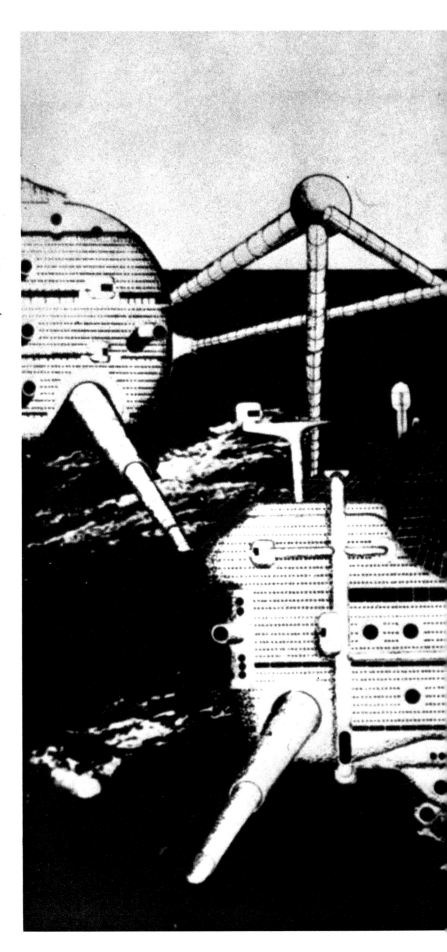

TWENTY-FIRST-CENTURY SPACE COLONIES

Wheellike space colonies orbiting between the earth and the moon are Dr. Gerard K. O'Neill's concept for the future. With NASA and Princeton University experts, and with the Ames/Stanford University Summer Study on Space Colonization, O'Neill has proposed such settlements which are made of moon and asteroid materials and could be manufactured in space using solar power. Gravity would be produced by centrifugal force of rotation of the wheel around its axis, and days, nights, and seasons would result from sunlight on outside mirrors.

ROGER C. FERRI, CORPORATE SKYSCRAPER FOR MADISON SQUARE

Right and far right: "The skyscraper is conceived as an active civic monument in New York, integrating the corporate goals of power and influence, the communal aspiration of shared amenity, and the individual's need for a setting that fosters and supports his sensient explorations.

The tower is built to the maximum floor area allowed under present zoning law. It maintains the street wall for eleven stories, then sets back to receive a mountainscape assembled from bedrock excavated from the building site. The landscape would be planted with flora native to the Hudson Valley region, and populated with fauna hardy to captivity, such as birds, fish, rabbits, and deer.

A public restaurant occupies the level of the first setback. At each intermediate office floor, the staff workspace overlooks a constantly changing tableau of wilderness and dense metropolis. Every office floor has direct staff access to the outdoor landscape" (Ferri, 1976).

PAOLO SOLERI, ARCOSANTI

Born in 1919, the architect Paolo Soleri first came to the United States from his native Italy in 1947. For a brief period he worked for Frank Lloyd Wright at the two Taliesins and then returned to Italy, where he devoted his time to building a ceramics factory. In 1954 he again came to the United States, but this time to settle in Scottsdale, Arizona, where he established another ceramics works. Since then Soleri has become known for his visionary designs called arcologies, a contraction of the words "ar-chitecture" and "ecology." As the name implies, his arcologies are space-age megastructures that concentrate all social life in urban complexes, returning to nature the lands once occupied and despoiled by our cities and villages.

Below: Hexahedron Arcology, population 170,000.

Right: Asteromo Arcology, population 70,000.

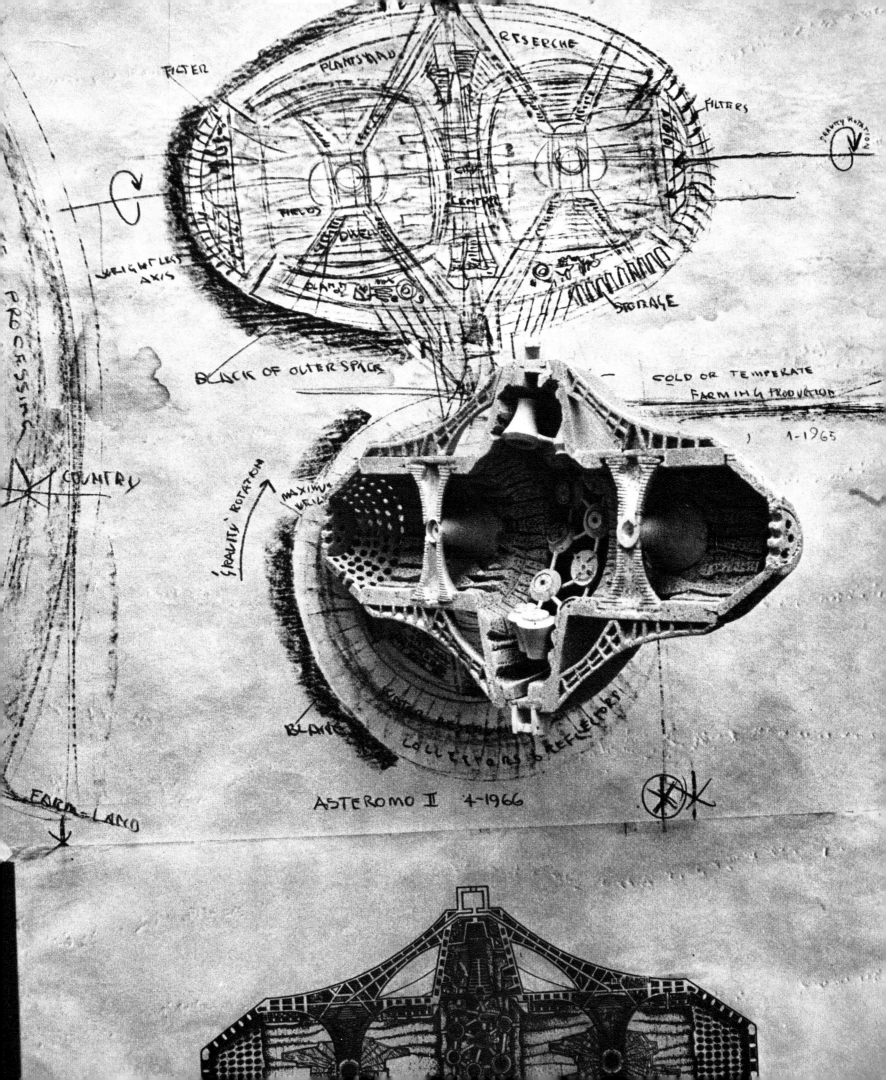

Since 1965 Soleri has been working to realize an arcology, although necessarily on a reduced scale. With the help of dedicated students and followers, he has been building Arcosanti near his home and factory outside Scottsdale. Guided by the philosophy of the French Jesuit Teilhard de Chardin, Soleri seeks to make Arcosanti embody, in his words, a "conception of the individual as part of an encompassing structure of civilization."

TAUT AND FINSTERLIN

Bruno Taut and Hermann Finsterlin were prominent among the Expressionists who turned to visionary art under the impact of the German turmoil in 1918. Already established as an architect before World War I, Bruno Taut was a founder of the Arbeitsrat für Kunst, which proclaimed: "Art should no longer be a luxury for the few but must reach and gladden the masses." Taut and Finsterlin contributed works of urbanistic fantasy to the Exhibition of Unknown Artists organized in Berlin in 1919.

Bruno Taut dreamed of glass structures and in his Building Site Seen from Mount Generoso, a sketch from his volume Alpine Architektur (1919), he portrays a vision of the Alps blanketed with crystalline glass structures that have the mystical power to liberate all who behold it.

A painter rather than an architect, Finsterlin created designs that lie somewhere between "the crystalline and the amorphous." As indicated by these drawings, his forms are painterly and exist outside the realm of functional practicality.

Top, opposite: Hermann Finsterlin, Museum, drawing.

Below: Bruno Taut, Building Site Seen from Mount Generoso, sketch.

Bottom, opposite: Hermann Finsterlin, House of Worship, drawing.

FREDERICK J. KIESLER, THE ENDLESS HOUSE

A brilliant, inventive product of Vienna of the 1920s, Kiesler (1892-1965) continued his search for new shapes and techniques in America. This model of the Endless House dates from 1958, but its origin comes from 1924. In his own words: "While the concept of the house does not advocate, a 'return to nature,' it certainly does encourage a more natural way of living, and a greater independence from our . . . automative way of life." Concrete was the material best adapted for this new construction principle.

HAUS-RUCKER-CO, THE RIGID DIGIT, NUREMBERG

Right and far right: The Rigid Digit, a 12-meter-high inflated finger that points the way from the Nuremberg airport to the city, may owe a debt to Pop imagery. It was raised in November 1971 by the Viennese design team Haus-Rucker-Co, and symbolizes the last sign of human life on earth after pollution has driven everyone to live in underground cities.

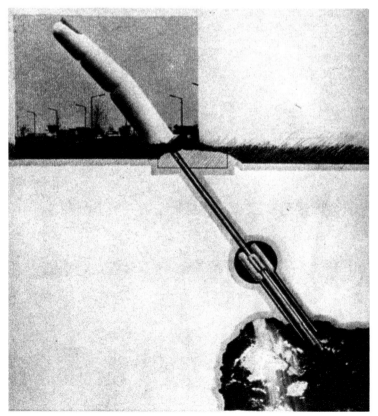

MAHARAJA SAWAI JAI SINGH II, OBSERVATORY

Here and following page: India is a land of unexpected contrasts, and some of the most delightful are to be found in Jaipur, the famous city built of pink sandstone in the desert of Rajasthan. For here a visitor on his way to see the palace built by the Rajputs in the eighteenth century will suddenly encounter what seems to be a modern sculpture garden filled with structures resembling a science-fiction set. Not "visionary" in the strict sense, these in fact are astronomical instruments built in 1734 by Maharaja Sawai Jai Singh II, who planned the city of Jaipur. From 1699 to his death in 1743 Jai Singh II ruled over the principality of Amber. A scholar as well as a statesman,

he early on showed a strong interest in mathematics and astronomy. In the course of his studies he concluded that Ptolemy's calculations in his Syntaxis *were inaccurate because they were derived from the use of relatively small-scale instruments. Jai Singh then decided to build monumental, astronomical instruments of stone that would reduce measuring error. His observatories were located in Jaipur, Delhi, Mathura (destroyed), Varanasi, and Ujjain, and each contained five basic instrument types. Time has unfortunately taken its toll of these impressive structures, but the Jaipur observatory remains in reasonably good condition.*

Rasjivalaya-Yantra, Jaipur.

Left: Samrat-Yantra, Jaipur.

Nadjivalaya-Yantra, Jaipur.

Samrat-Yantra, New Delhi.

Misjra-Yantra, New Delhi.

View from the Samrat-Yantra, Ujjain.

AUROVILLE

Under construction since 1968 near Pondicherry, the capital of the former French enclave in India, Auroville is a growing commune dedicated to realizing the spiritual vision of the famous Indian mystic philosopher Sri Aurobindo. When completed, the city is expected to have some 50,000 inhabitants, who will live communally according to the precepts of the system of spiritual discipline that Aurobindo called Integral Yoga. Auroville grew out of the ashram, or spiritual community, which Sri Aurobindo and his consort Mira Richard established in 1926.

Overall view of the construction.

Model of the city.

ANTONIO GAUDÍ, SAGRADA FAMILIA

Antonio Gaudí was born in 1852 in the Catalan town of Reus. While still a student at the school of architecture in Barcelona, the young Gaudí was deeply influenced by the nationalist, revivalist philosophy then espoused by many Catalans. For inspiration, Gaudí looked to the structure and geometries of medieval art and the architectural ideas of Viollet-le-Duc. Gaudí became devoutly religious, and conceived of architecture as deified nature.

A major work was the Church of the Sagrada Familia (Sacred Family) in Barcelona. When he assumed control over the project in 1883, Gaudí began to transform the original Neo-Gothic design into his own structural and sculpturesque style. Work on the Sagrada Familia absorbed much of Gaudí's attention up to his accidental death in 1926. Thus the church shows the different phases in Gaudí's creative career. Some elements have a Neo-Gothic flavor, some combine the exuberance of Art Nouveau with early Gothic traditionalism, and the towers are even more fanciful and hint at Cubist influence. On the pinnacles of the towers are colored glass mosaics, a combination of prisms and other geometric forms with the words "Hosanna! Sanctus! Gloria!"

Construction of the still-unfinished Sagrada Familia was—and still is—to be financed solely through donations rather than through regular church income. Thus, for Gaudí the act of building was an act of piety.

ANTONIO GAUDÍ, CASA BATLLÓ

In 1904 Gaudí was commissioned to design a new façade for the Casa Batlló, an apartment building in Barcelona. Upon the façade Gaudí projected what appear to be teeming, organic forms crystallized in ceramic and sculpture. The iridescent tiles recall the foam of a breaking wave, while the ironwork of the balconies looks like masks. The roof appears to be an enormous ceramic dragon, its scaly feet hanging over the eaves, which symbolizes St. George, the patron saint of Barcelona.

ANTONIO GAUDÍ,
GÜELL PARK

Güell Park is situated on a barren rise behind the center of Barcelona, offering a full view of the city and the Sagrada Familia. In 1900 Eusebio Güell commissioned Gaudí to create a village within a landscape setting akin to an English garden. During the next fourteen years Gaudí built three of the sixty houses he had planned, as well as viaducts and galleries on the rugged terrain of the park. These viaducts and park benches meander through the park like a caterpillar. The benches are constructed of the colorful ceramic mosaics that Gaudí so loved and they resemble Cubist collage. Gaudí made the park his home from 1906 until shortly before his death in 1926. Later, the park was opened to the public and it still is very much enjoyed today.

Right: Mosaic benches.

Below: Columns of the viaduct.

ANTONIO GAUDÍ, CASA MILÁ

Designed by Gaudí in 1906, Casa Milá in Barcelona is popularly known as La Pedrera *(the quarry) because of its monolithic, rock-hewn appearance. Iron supports the stonework that projects from the facade in many places, and the balconies are made of metal beams with glass flooring which allows the sunlight to fall directly on the windows or balcony below. Each floor plan is different, but every apartment shares the same curving ceilings, door and window frames, and furniture. On the roof, the chimney pots and the pinnacles are rendered in bizarre, supernatural forms, encrusted with colorful mosaics and sculpted into playful and grotesque shapes, based on geometric spirals. A statue of the Virgin de la Gracia was originally designed to grace the top of the building, but its patron decided not to add the sculpture after the outpouring of anticlerical sentiment during the Barcelona uprising of 1909. Disappointed, the devout Gaudí lost interest in the project and left the Casa Milá to his assistants to complete.*

RUDOLF STEINER, GOETHEANUM

Rudolf Steiner was an admirer of Goethe and named his school and meetinghouse in Dornach, Switzerland, the Goetheanum, where he propagated his educational and philosophical ideas. The founder of anthroposophy, Steiner believed that the arts were a means of gaining an understanding of the universe. The construction of the first Goetheanum was started in 1913, but the building was destroyed by fire in 1922. In 1925, the year Steiner died, the second Goetheanum was begun and it was completed in 1928.

The building's various elements suggest human organs—brain, heart, lungs—and through them one is led from the physical world outside to the interior where music, dance, theater, and architecture combine to enlighten the visitor and deepen his spiritual world. Metamorphosis is a key concept in the Goetheanum. Shapes and textures flow together and they are used symbolically in accordance with Steiner's philosophy.

Above: Front view of the Goetheanum.

Below: The first Goetheanum, 1913–22, demolished by fire.

Opposite: The Boilerhouse, 1914–15.

House Duldeck.

Stairwell in the Goetheanum.

Detail of balustrade and door ornaments.

Detail of the roof.

130

ERIC MENDELSOHN, EINSTEIN TOWER

Mendelsohn, the great German-American architect (1887–1953), made many visionary, utopian sketches based on futuristic forms that originated in the trenches of World War I. The famous Einstein Tower of the Astro- *Physical Institute of Potsdam (1921) was designed to be constructed in flowing concrete, but was in actuality built of brick with a stucco coating.*

SUPERSTUDIO, THE CONTINUOUS MONUMENT

Superstudio, an avant-garde architectural group from Florence, Italy, designed these visionary collages. The Continuous Monument, huge geometric shapes stretching over entire cities and countrysides, will house the world's population. This is the architecture of the future, the only alternative to nature! Left: Here is how Superstudio describes the Architectural Model for Total Urbanization, New New York (1969):

New York for example. A superstructure passes over the Hudson and the point of the peninsula joining Brooklyn and New Jersey. And a second perpendicular structure for expansion. All the rest is Central Park. This is sufficient to hold the entire built-up volume of Manhattan. A bunch of ancient skyscrapers, preserved in memory of a time when cities were built with no single plan. . . . And from the Bay, we see New New York arranged by the Continuous Monument into a great plain of ice, clouds or sky.

SITE PROJECTS

SITE is an organization composed of architects, artists, and technicians with the purpose of exploring new concepts of architecture and public spaces. Wishing to eliminate set conventions, SITE uses the term "de-architecture" to describe its philosophy, and its work is an endeavor to introduce humor, fragmentation, ambiguity, and disorder into its designs. SITE has built these retail showrooms for the Best Products Company, a large catalog-showroom merchandiser.

Top: Notch Project, Sacramento, California, with a "Wandering Wall" unit that moves 40 feet in either direction (1977).

Middle: Tilt Showroom, Towson, Maryland (1978).

Right: Peeling Project, Richmond, Virginia (1972).

Far right: Indeterminate Facade, Houston, Texas (1975).

A Parking Lot Project for Los Angeles, California (1976) by SITE, this proposal suggests rolling a parking lot over the warehouse. Thus two eyesores are transformed into an urban fantasy.

UNUSUAL MATERIALS

George Plumb, top edge of bottle wall

GEORGE PLUMB

A carpenter by trade, George Plumb works with different materials in different styles. His bottle house in Duncan, British Columbia, is composed of bottles of all kinds, shapes, and sizes. He began work on this glass castle in 1963 and after it had been completed other structures in glass were created, among them models of the Taj Mahal and the Leaning Tower of Pisa. So far Plumb has used over 180,000 bottles. Here are bottle details and a view of his studio.

ELIS STENMAN

In Pigeon Cove, Massachusetts, Elis Stenman and his wife built and furnished their house from newspapers. Stenman experimented with rolling the newspapers in a way that would not destroy the print and that used no glue or varnish. Thus the resulting rolls became a wood substitute and were used like Lincoln Logs to make chairs, tables, lamps, a clock. Even the fireplace was made of these newspaper logs. Stenman and his wife began their work on the paper house in 1922 and when Stenman died in 1942, about 100,000 newspapers had been used.

CHICO

In the Gate of Haarlem, one of the entrance gates to Amsterdam, lives the young Mexican Chico, who for years has been creating his plastic palace—everything covered and draped in plastic.

DAVID BROWN

Here and overleaf: David Brown's Glass House in Boswell, British Columbia, and the bridges, towers, and walls are made of square embalming fluid bottles, all of them eight inches long and three inches square. The bottles are laid in mortar like bricks, though the glass is harder to work with.

In 1952, after his retirement from the funeral business that he had been in most of his life, Brown started building. His house drew so much attention from the public that he had little privacy. Ever since his death in 1970, the house has become a museum which his son administers.

MIKE REYNOLDS

Recycling! A critical approach to the energy problem has led to the study of possibilities for recycling. Aluminum cans turned out to be usable building stones; bottles and old car tires were also possible.

The American Mike Reynolds experimented with many kinds of materials. He built his own house of bottles, old wood, and discarded automobile tires in Taos, New Mexico.

Far left: Preliminary tire walls.

Bottom: Next, plastered tires.

Left: One of the finished houses.

Mike Reynolds, Adobe House with Cans, Taos, New Mexico.

BOAT INTO HOUSE

This house made from a boat is in Copenhagen, Denmark, in the free town of Christiania. In 1971, inhabitants of the city took illegal possession of this territory inside Copenhagen's old walls. Until a year earlier it had been used by the Danish army. The free area was first transformed into playgrounds for children and later, abandoned buildings were turned into residences.

GODFRIED GABRIEL, BOTTLERAMA

Here and overleaf: Godfried Gabriel was born in 1891 in the Ukraine (USSR). After a period of imprisonment in Siberia, he came to Canada in 1930 where he found a job as a construction worker. Upon his retirement when he was 60, he began to decorate his garage in Oliver, British Columbia, with lamps and bottles. He was not able to obtain permission from the local authorities to continue to build with bottles, and he therefore purchased a plot of land outside Oliver, half a mile south of Vaseaux Lake on Highway 97. Here the Bottlerama was created over a period of eighteen years: a sequence of structures made out of bottles and car headlights along with a cloister and several monuments. When Gabriel eventually completes his work, the entire place will be paved with bottles.

Back of storage place.

Front of storage place.

His garage in Oliver.

Monument for the gnomes.

GRANDMA PRISBREY, BOTTLE VILLAGE

Left, below, and overleaf: Grandma Prisbrey was born in 1895, and in 1955 she and her husband went to live in a trailer in Santa Susana, California. But her trailer was too small for her grandchildren and ultimately too small for her many collections, which she had been gathering for a long time. The first of her thirteen houses was built because the trailer could not hold her growing collection of 2,000 pencils.

Besides her Pencil House, there is also the Rumpus Room, the Leaning Tower of Pisa, the School House, Shell House, Blue Bottle House, Round House, Cleopatra's Bedroom, Doll House, Little Chapel, Cabana, Little Hut, and Thatched House. Among her other structures: a wishing well, shrine, TV tube wall, sanctuary wall, fountain, pyramid planter, and doll's head planter.

These houses were built with bottles because it was cheaper than building with concrete blocks. By the time she had finished the Bottle Village, she had used about one million bottles, most of which she had collected from the city dump, as she did other discarded materials such as dolls, medical supplies, plumbing fixtures, car headlights, license plates, and many more. The only supplies she bought were sand and cement, roofing paper, and wood for studs.

Left: Detail of paved road.

Below: The School House.

Card House.

View toward the Round House.

Cleopatra's Bedroom.

Rumpus Room.

The Little Chapel.

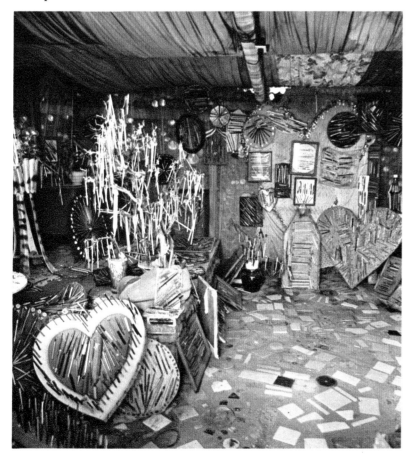

The Pencil House.

The headlight-covered shrines.

159

BALDASARE FORESTIERE

Here and overleaf: Baldasare Forestiere (born 1879) came to this country in 1902 from Messina, Sicily. His family had been citrus growers, but the heat in Fresno, California, was too much for citrus growing and his land was rocky and poor. To escape the heat, he hollowed out a room under the ground, chipping out the rock. He made no plan, just dug. He dug one hundred rooms and patios spread under seven acres of land. Each one had a skylight or a hole open to the surface, and light and water necessary to sustain the fruit trees he planted below. His living area consisted of a living room, dining room, kitchen, and two bedrooms. Once he arranged for a woman to stay and see if she could adjust to underground living. She left.

When Forestiere died in 1946 there was also a 700-foot-long tunnel that was to lead to an underground Italian restaurant.

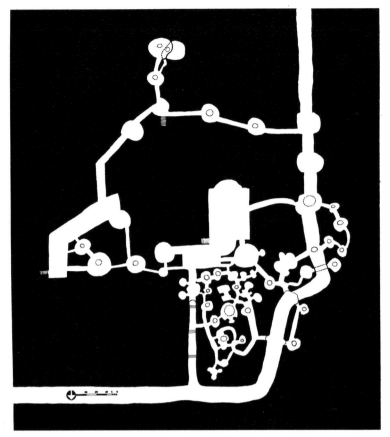

Plan of the underground space.

View through one of the corridors.

Kitchen.

Bedroom.

Bathroom.

INTERIORS-EXTERIORS

Junker House, Lemgo

JUNKER HOUSE

Here and overleaf: Karl Junker, born in Lemgo, Germany, learned the trade of cabinetmaker, then attended the Munich Art Academy. From 1890 until his death in 1912, he worked day and night covering his house with wood-carvings both inside and out.

On the outside of this strange house, Junker nailed lengthwise and crosswise borders to the beams, over and over again, with bumps and humps. On the inside, all walls and ceilings are loaded with carved "ghosts." Everywhere one looks there are fantastic forms, and it is frequently difficult to know what they are representing— man, animal, tree, or flower. Among them are distorted ornaments and wall paintings.

All the rooms are "furnished," and all the tables, chairs, cupboards, chests, and beds are made, carved, and decorated by Junker in the same fantastic way. He himself never lived in any of these, preferring a small attic in the house.

His studio.

Living room.

Model for his new house.

His bedroom.

Entrance hall.

Some of his sculptured panels.

Detail of a stepladder.

Front of the house.

Stepladder.

168

VICTOR V

Left: In Amsterdam, he mockingly called his house the seat of the Société Culturelle d'Excellence d'Amsterdam.

FRED BURNS

Fred Burns calls his house "something different." He built it with driftwood off the beach, with old rusty nails, and the remnants of leftover paint.

Burns was born in Maine in 1898. He has lived there all his life as a hunter, trapper, and guide except for his period of service in World War I. For the last thirty-six years he has lived on the harbor in Belfast. A nearby chicken factory and good fishing provide him and his dogs with food.

MS. G.

Top: Born in 1898, Ms. G. lives in Nesles-la-Gilberde (Seine-et-Marne, France). For unknown reasons, Ms. G. does not want his full name to be used. He still fears his neighbors' reactions to him and his work, and he has built his house without ever having requested a building permit. Since the death of his wife, Ms. G. lives alone in the painted, plastered, and almost completed house. The inte-

rior and exterior are adorned with fantastic images, self-portraits, and patriotic scenes, which seem to testify to his love of his country.

Left: Doorbell.

Right: Rainspout.

DECORATED EXTRAVAGANZAS

Exterior decorations serve to extend the personality of the owner and/or builder into the outside world.

Left: The nightclub in Paris, L'Enfer, with its bizarre frontal ornamentation no longer exists.

Top, right: Jean-Jacques Lequeu (1757–1825?) designed this hermit's hut with four tree-columns. While garden pavilions of bark-covered logs were fairly common, here the architect outdid his contemporaries by adding more than the usual gimmickries.

Bottom: A contemporary house decorated with cement trees and branches is in Lorraine, France.

CIGARBAND HOUSE

N. Molenaar worked for about sixteen years on the interior of his house in Volendam, Holland, where he used some seven million cigarbands to make his mosaic. His images are views of the world's masterpieces such as Big Ben in London, the Piazza San Marco in Venice, the Statue of Liberty, and others. The house is now a little museum on top of a souvenir shop.

CAPUCHIN CEMETERY

The Cave dei Cappuccini, or Cemetery of the Capuchins, is on the Via Veneto in Rome. The church Santa Maria della Concezione, also called Santa Maria dei Cappuccini, was built in 1626, and the four vaults hold the bones of approximately 4,000 monks.

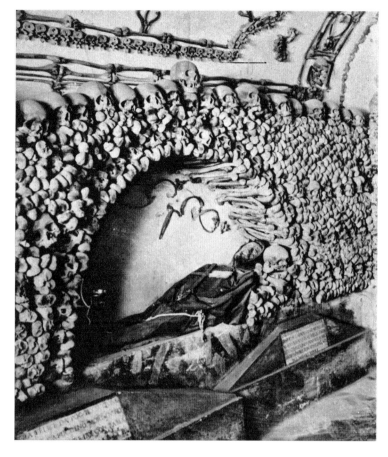

CHARNEL HOUSE

This little building in Portugal, which stands next to a church, is completely lined on the inside with skulls and bones of the deceased parishioners.

ST. EOM

Edward Owen Martin was born in 1908 in Buena Vista, Georgia. When he retired, leaving New York City in 1957, it was to return to his Georgia home. Signing all of his paintings and creative works St. Eom, he began in earnest his works of art in building materials, cement, and stucco. He has built a large and very colorful compound decorated with geometric designs, figures, and reptiles, "using the influence of the ancient rituals and arts," as he says.

MARCEL DHIÈVRE, PETIT PARIS

*Top and overleaf: Almost all his life Marcel Dhièvre oper-
ated a small clothing store behind which he lived with his
wife. After his retirement, he began to decorate the facade
of his house in brilliant colors and this occupied him for
twelve years. In the village street of Saint-Dizier, Petit*
*Paris was created: an assemblage of flowers and plants,
copies of well-known monuments such as the Arch of
Triumph and the Eiffel Tower, and scenes from the fables
of La Fontaine. Dhièvre died in 1977.*

FATHER MATTHIAS WERNERUS

Right and below: Born in 1873 in Germany, Father Matthias came to the United States in 1904. In 1916 he was appointed pastor of the Holy Ghost Parish in Dickeyville, Wisconsin. Ten years later, he began work on his Grotto in Holy Ghost Park. He shaped steel, covering it with wire, then concrete, and finally with primarily shell mosaics. He also used stones, marbles, gems, glass, and whatever his parishioners brought him.

Far right, top: A thatched cottage near Kildare, Ireland, has Irish symbols—harp, shamrock, Celtic cross— executed in seashells.

Far right, bottom: A house in Dives-sur-Mer, Calvados, France, with mosaic decorations and a monument to Sputnik.

182

RAYMOND ISIDORE

Raymond Isidore, born in Chartres, France, in 1900, worked for a short period of time in a metal foundry. For many years he maintained the city's cemeteries as an employee of the city of Chartres. Toward the end of the twenties he bought land on the outskirts of Chartres where he built a house for himself, his wife, and children. He started to expand it with a chapel, then a second house,

and decorated them with pieces of glass he found every-where in the surroundings. On a second plot bought after the war, Isidore built a barn against the house and his "Tombeau de l'esprit" (Tomb of the Spirit).

Isidore's work shows him as a man who felt misplaced in society, but who derived strength from his faith and his love for nature.

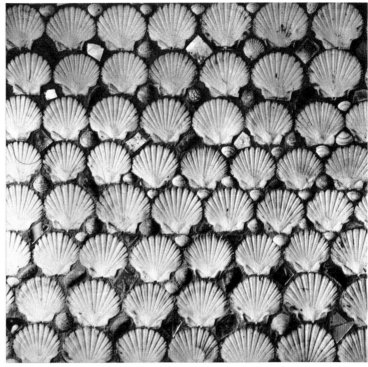

ROBERT VASSEUR

Left, above, and overleaf: In about 1952 Robert Vasseur, a retired milkman, began to decorate his house and garden in Louviers, France, with mosaics. By now, the interior and exterior of the house have been almost completely covered with mosaics. In addition the garden is crowded with all kinds of mosaic objects and Vasseur still con- *tinues with the work. Some of the materials are obtained from his neighbors and also from community garbage dumps. Much of the decoration is from seashells, since Louviers is about two hours from the sea. Vasseur makes very precise mosaics, most of them in geometric, abstract designs, not in representational pictures.*

TROMPE L'OEIL

Painting scenes on outside or inside walls that trick the observer into believing he is somewhere else or that he is seeing something else has been used for many centuries. Trompe l'oeil—deceive the eye.

Below: A painted building and a painted street in Venice, Los Angeles, California. The work is typical of artists' groups, the best known being the Los Angeles Fine Arts Squadron.

Right: This fake house with fake windows is in the Rue Quincampoix, Paris, near the Centre Pompidou.

Above: A well-known mural painter of Manchester, England, Walter Kershaw brightened up a street with his vivid mural Inside Out, which does indeed show the domestic life of a typical family including someone in the bathtub.

Left: Look again! Richard Haas created this "building" at 112–114 Prince Street in the Soho section of New York City. Nothing is real.

PRINCE OF PALAGONIA

Overleaf: In addition to his stone monsters (pp. 60, 61), the prince had the ceiling of his Sicilian villa painted with architectural balustrades and cornices, animals, and flowers that were delightfully deceiving.

IRIAL VETS, REPLICA OF THE SISTINE CHAPEL

Born in 1908, the Frenchman Irial Vets started out in life as a shoemaker, but later became a restaurateur. One day Vets noticed in the newspaper an advertisement placing on sale a church in the nearby village of Broglie. He purchased the provincial church with the intention of replicating here the great Renaissance masterpieces adorning the Sistine Chapel in Rome. Every winter Vets retires to the church to cover its walls with copies of the frescoes of Michelangelo, Perugino, Ghirlandaio, and the other masters. Vets has also added sculpture, including his own waiting tomb.

FRA ANDREA POZZO, IL GESÙ

Begun in 1682, these remarkable trompe l'oeil frescoes in Rome make a plain barrel vault appear as if it had arches, cornices, and other three-dimensional figures. When one moves along the corridor of St. Ignatius' rooms, the elaborate architectural tricks become nothing but abstract configurations.

Stairs leading nowhere.

A storeroom.

Left: Door leading to a two-story drop through a skylight.

WINCHESTER MANSION

Here and overleaf: Sarah L. Winchester was the heiress to the Winchester rifle fortune. After her child and her husband died, she consulted a spiritualist who told her that she was being harassed by the ghosts of people who had been killed by the Winchester rifle.

In order to ward them off, she was advised to buy another house far away from New Haven, and to continue adding more rooms to the new house to confuse the ghosts. Thus she bought a house with nine rooms in San Jose, California, and from 1884 on she continued to add more and more new rooms until her death in 1922. During that time, about thirty bricklayers, plasterers, and carpenters worked on the house seven days a week including Christmas, so that the work was not interrupted for a moment.

When she died at the age of 85, there were about 160 rooms and the house was full of ghost traps: a staircase leading to the ceiling so that the ghost would bump his head; doors with only a blank wall behind them; storerooms; trick closets; and bell towers to signal spirits at night.

CLARENCE SCHMIDT, WOODSTOCK, NEW YORK

Born in 1897, Clarence Schmidt received training as a plasterer and bricklayer. In the late 1930s he built his first house, Journey's End, a kind of log cabin, tarred, and decorated with fragments of glass. He lived there a few years and then started building a second house, a House of Mirrors, a gigantic assemblage of refuse, old window and door frames, and other wood. The walls were pasted over with aluminum foil or painted with aluminum paint. In 1968, when this house burned down, it had seven floors.

Almost immediately after the fire, Schmidt started all over. The result, however, was never as impressive as the House of Mirrors because three years after the first fire this structure, Mark II, also burned down. Schmidt is now in a rest home. Only ruins remain of his work, although his son Michael has tried to integrate his own sculpture into the remains.

OUTCROPPINGS

Right: As an answer to the housing problems in Geneva, Marcel Lachat built this bubble with the help of friends. It is more than 30 feet square and weighs 600 pounds. In addition, he had the good fortune of having a daughter born in it.

Below: Big Ben of London and the Leaning Tower of Pisa are balanced on the rooftop of this house.

Far right: A bay window in the form of a ship is in the Schildersstraat in Antwerp, Belgium.

CHIEF ROLLING THUNDER

Above: Chief Rolling Thunder in the Mountains, born in 1911, is a Creek Indian and had worked as a trapper, trimmer, gold miner, and logger before World War II. A tank driver in the U.S. Army, he was wounded and has been living on a veteran's disability pension ever since.

In 1965 he began building a house for his family in Imlay, Nevada, at the foot of Thunder Mountain where the Paiute Indians used to celebrate their sun dance. Fourteen years later, the house has three floors and nine rooms. It has been completely built out of refuse and has been decorated with sculptures of Indian warriors, medicine men, and daughters of the headman. In the center, a standing woman and her children raise their arms high to the sun.

VIC MOORE, THE MOORAGE

Right: Vic Moore for some seventeen years has been an art consultant in the Pullman school system, state of Washington, and now teaches art at Pullman High. Six years ago he decided to pursue a master's degree in fine arts at Washington State University. Building The Moorage, his castle near Pullman, was to be his thesis. It is a weird conglomerate of junk, car doors, chunks of metal from old combine machines, old bedsteads, and road signs.

Moore says that his creation is "a big assemblage and it has absolutely no practical, utilitarian function like architecture . . . no motive for existence. It is so absurd, that's what made it a labor of love." The Moorage is not yet finished, though Vic did receive his master's in fine arts.

CHOMO, VILLAGE OF PRELUDE ART

At his secluded cottage in the woods near Achères-la-Forêt, France, Chomo (Roger Chomeaux) has been creating what he calls a "village d'art pré-ludien" (Village of Prelude Art)—an assemblage of structures, paintings, sculptures, and large musical instruments intended to anticipate a better future. Chomo works with materials he finds: wood from the forest and refuse of plastic, metal, and glass. His statues made from scorched wood are housed in a sanctuary constructed of wooden poles and chicken wire that has been covered with plaster of Paris. Using the same technique, Chomo has also built a "church of the poor," which is filled with his experimental sculptures, and a cavelike "refuge," incorporating refuse materials assembled in free improvisation. In 1977 Chomo began to construct a cathedral mainly out of old bicycles, which probably never will be completed because he began the work without any structurally sound design in mind.

DROP CITY

Right: In Colorado, a community of hippies called Drop City came into being in 1965. The nucleus was formed by three people who had escaped from society and who tried to give shape to their ideal here. Under the influence of the architect Buckminster Fuller, they enthusiastically tackled the construction of domes out of materials discarded by our consumer society.

HOUSEBOAT COMMUNITY

Above and far right: In Sausalito, California, there is a floating community of houseboats inhabited mostly by artists. Authorities have been trying to dislodge the houseboaters to make room for high-rise apartments, but the Waldo Point residents have made a strong stand.

The houseboat Madonna (right) by Chris Roberts, one of the many vessels that made up the community, had been declared a work of art by the state of California before it burned.

GARDENS

Hen and her eggs, a 300-year-old English yew being trimmed. Overleaf: Gabriel's garden

ROMANO GABRIEL

A wooden garden of flowers, faces, and carousels more than a house high—this is the garden of Romano Gabriel in Eureka, California.

Gabriel was a gardener who came from Italy in 1913, but "Eureka is bad place for flowers," he told Jan Wampler, author of the book, All Their Own. *So he built his own garden out of a longing for the exuberance of Italian flora and with the wood from fruit crates. He did so for thirty years until the boxes were no longer made of wood.*

Gabriel died in 1977, and on the day of his death the California State Arts Council designated his garden an important piece of folk art.

GEORGE PLUMB *His Glass Castle in Canada (see pp. 138–41) extends into his garden.*

BOMARZO

Here and overleaf: The garden of Bomarzo, built by Prince Corrado Orsini, called Vicino, is also known as the Sacro Bosco (Sacred Wood). The garden came of Prince Corrado's love for Princess Giulia Farnese, his wife.

Legend has it that a number of Turkish prisoners of war built the colossal statues, but it is more probable that a group of Italian sculptors worked for about ten years to carry out Count Vicino Orsini's commission. The architect was Pirro Ligorio, an archaeologist and painter, born in Naples in 1513. In Bomarzo, the inspiration of Vicino and Ligorio created a garden of huge stone bears, elephants, monsters, mermaids, giants, a leaning building, a temple, and many more.

PIERRE AVEZARD

Pierre Avezard, born in 1901, was a cowherd who built a fair in his backyard in Fay-aux-Loges. From 1938 on, he has for many years spent all his spare time on his garden, making a large complex of mechanized, moving objects out of discarded materials. His work is known as the merry-go-round.

AW BOON HAW, TIGER BALM GARDENS

Top, right, and overleaf: Aw Boon Haw, a Chinese, built Tiger Balm Gardens in Hong Kong (top) and in Singapore (right and overleaf). Once Mr. Aw was prohibited entrance to a park by a sign that read: "No entrance allowed to dogs and Chinese." So, much later, in the 1930s, when he had become a millionaire from the development of Tiger Balm, the world-famous muscle analgesic, he built these beautiful gardens, which are open to everyone. The statuary depicts mythical Chinese figures and various denizens of the earth and heaven.

不准入池
DO NOT ENTER

CAMILLE VIDAL, NOAH'S ARK

Above and right: A French bricklayer born in 1895, Camille Vidal stopped working at the age of 60. He tried to combat the emptiness of his retirement by reproducing, in his garden in Agde, France, objects and beings from his daily life, images from magazines, and many animals, thanks to which the garden was named Noah's Ark. Vidal later added portraits of some of his idols such as Clemenceau and Churchill, also of Adam and Eve. After his death, the garden fell into disrepair. Few statues remain.

DRIFTWOOD CHARLEY CASKIN

Far left, left: In 1947 the doctors said that Charles Caskin had only a short time to live unless he moved to a hot, dry climate. First he moved to the Death Valley area, and in 1960 he left for Yuma, Arizona, where Driftwood Charley's World of Lost Art was created. Caskin's memoirs and scenes from the Bible have been hacked out of the soft local stone and modeled in concrete.

R. GUITET

Left: The zoological sculpture garden of R. Guitet in Sauveterre-de-Guyenne, France shows animals, people, and three sages who hear no evil, see no evil, speak no evil.

SAMUEL PERRY DINSMOOR, GARDEN OF EDEN

Dinsmoor was born in 1843 and fought in the American Civil War. In 1905 he bought a small piece of land in Lucas, Kansas, on which to build his house and around it he created a Garden of Eden: a forest of trees, many Biblical figures, animals, and plants. The sculptures were made of concrete, molded when wet over chicken wire, and were lit up at night.

FERNAND CHATELAIN, THE CENTAURS

Left: Since 1965 Fernand Chatelain, a baker by profession, has been building fanciful sculptures in the garden of his home in Fye, France, a village near Alençon. His first structure was a miniature castle, which unfortunately was soon destroyed by vandals. Undaunted, Chatelain continued to build playful sculptural compositions, usually representing animal and human figures. Chatelain first fashions a skeleton out of wire, stuffs the core with crumpled paper, and plasters the frame with cement; when hardened, it is then painted.

FRED SMITH, CONCRETE PARK

Right and below: Fred Smith has spent fifty-six years of his life as a Wisconsin logger and pulpcutter. Shortly before 1949 he began to build his Concrete Park in Phillips, Wisconsin, with 203 glass-covered, concrete images. Other materials he used were bottles and plastic. These figures portray incidents from folklore, local history, and daily life, among which are the Statue of Liberty and what he inscribed "Statue freedom of Capitaldom."

ADOLPHE-JULIEN FOUÉRÉ

Adolphe-Julien Fouéré was born in 1842. A clergyman who led the life of a hermit, he lived in a small house near the village of Rothéneuf (on the coast of Brittany near St. Malo, France). From 1885 until his death in 1910 Fouéré sculpted the genealogy of the Rothéneufs into the rocks. They were a notorious local family of pirates, fishermen, and smugglers who controlled the entire Channel from the middle of the sixteenth century until after the French Revolution. Beasts and sea monsters are devouring this family.

HOWARD FINSTER, GARDEN OF PARADISE

Above: The Reverend Howard Finster is a retired preacher in Summerville, Georgia, where he began to build a Garden of Paradise in his backyard. It is built of objets trouvés *embedded in concrete, along with Bible verses, sometimes in mosaic.*

MARCEL LANDREAU

Right: Marcel Landreau was born in 1922. His greatest desire was to become a confectioner and create beautiful things sculpted in sugar. Instead, he became a baker around 1936.

In 1958 he began building his own small sculptures in Mantes, France: a fort, a mill, and some figures. In 1967 a cathedral was completed, and he added a bridal part, a hunting scene, a ballroom scene, and in 1974 one of his last big objects—Charlie Chaplin. Ever since, Landreau works mostly on separate pieces that can be moved. His garden is finished.

EDWARD LEEDSKALNIN, CORAL CASTLE

Left and below: All that Ed Leedskalnin built was in the hopes that his former fiancée, whom he called Sweet Sixteen and who jilted him, would find out how famous he had become and leave Latvia to join him.

Leedskalnin first settled near Florida City on the edge of the Everglades and began working on the coral rock, cutting out blocks to make a home. In the 1930s, a company made plans to build a subdivision, so he moved further north to Homestead, Florida, where he bought ten acres of land and started building Coral Castle. Among other things he built chairs, even rocking chairs, out of the coral rock, a table shaped like Florida, a coral rock telescope, and a moon fountain. Leedskalnin died in 1951 at the age of 64.

TOPIARY

The art of topiary—sculpting shrubs and trees into ornamental designs—is very ancient. For the Romans, this cut and trimmed greenery was perhaps an inexpensive substitute for the marble and stone sculptures that the wealthy displayed in their gardens. By the time Pliny the Younger in the first century A.D. built his famous villa and garden, topiary art was well advanced. Indeed, Pliny described realistic scenes cut out of boxwood and cypress, including whole fleets of ships and hunting scenes. In nineteenth-century England, topiary was a much-loved art, but splendid shapes can be found in many countries.

Far left: A yew cut into an umbrella shape in France.

Top left: A castle and duck of cut yews.

Top right: Teatime on a privet table, in privet chairs! Over a period of some thirty years, Mr. and Mrs. Mitchell have shaped this suite of furniture at Houldsworth-terrace, Newmarket, England.

Bottom: An immense trimmed bird of box in Holland.

In Tulcan, Ecuador, a remarkable topiary garden and cemetery were fashioned from cyprus trees. Azael Franco Guerrero was born in 1899 in nearby El Angel, and he has for the last forty years created and lovingly cared for this curious assemblage. Faces of historical South American and Inca heroes stand side by side with obelisks, pyramids, rounded arches, caryatids, and animals—shapes taken from Egyptian, Oriental, and Indian village cultures. Some 200 cyprus pieces fill the cemetery's 400 square meters.

Franco Guerrero has great affection for his plants and the death of one is a tragedy in his life. The 81-year-old agronomist finds it hard to continue the necessary daily snipping and pruning, and some younger men are being trained to carry on his work.

Not real Scottie dogs, but they seem alive in this garden.

HERMAN RUSCH, PRAIRIE MOON GARDEN

Left: Born in 1886, Herman Rusch was a farmer all his life. When he was 71, he had an opportunity to rent an old dance pavilion, the Prairie Moon in Cochrane, Wisconsin, which had stood abandoned. Deciding to improve things a little, Rusch built a number of concrete arches. While he was building, the idea took shape to leave something behind for posterity. The work on this project dispelled the boredom of old age and resulted in the Prairie Moon Museum and Garden. Everything that Rusch constructed was built of concrete into which pieces of glass and pottery were pressed for decoration.

Among other things on his site are to be found a concrete flower planter, a stone birdhouse, a Hindu temple, a watch tower, a round spiral, and a dinosaur.

FOLLIES

Follies means foolishness. Strange structures of no use, not quite buildings, they are often put in fields, parks, or gardens so as to extend their beauty and complete the view. Follies are mostly British creations, although they do exist on the Continent, and most of them were erected between 1720 and 1850. Some of them are quite small and fit well into private gardens. Others are large and indicate the builder's eccentricity.

Left: A nonfunctional, inventive tower—a contemporary folly—was erected by Norman Van Praag near his home in Putten, Holland. He is 71 years old and has been building since the 1960s: two towers, copies of the Temple of Apollo and the seat of the Delphic Oracle, and a triumphal arch. His work is very simple, built of concrete elements that have been poured into fluted, plastic molds.

Middle: Cone in Barwick Park, Somerset, England. George Messiter probably had it built on his estate around 1820.

Right: This eighteenth-century pyramid, set in a romantic garden in the Désert du Retz, France, was used for storing ice from the Alps and was intended as a tomb. The design may be attributed to its owner, the Chevalier Racine de Monville, or to the architect François Barbier.

Above: British Admiral George Anson had James "Athenian" Stuart build this triumphal arch to commemorate his around-the-world voyage in 1740–44. It is a replica of the Arch of Hadrian in Athens and was erected in 1761 on his estate Shugborough Hall in Staffordshire, England.

Bottom: Oban McCraig's folly is in Argyll, Scotland.

Mad Jack Fuller's Folly, Sugar Loaf, erected in the early nineteenth century in Dallington, England.

LIST OF ARTISTS

PHOTO CREDITS

ACKNOWLEDGMENTS

The authors would like to thank the following people for their contributions to this book, with special thanks to the Westland-Utrecht Bank, which helped us with a grant.

Ondine Buytendorp, Mr. Tettelaar, Prof. Juan Bassegoda Nonell, Juan O'Gorman, Edward James, Maria and Plutarco Gastelum, Rachel, Jurgen Steinke, Ton Boersma, Niki de Saint Phalle, Tinguely, Jim Turrell, Elisabeth Turrell, Michael Jost, Toutchka von Goldschmidt, Jana Claverie, Mien and Dick Elffers, Chomo, SITE, Catharine Dreyfus, Pat Rotter, Andrea Gout, Walt von Praag, Mrs. Plumb, Godfried Gabriel, Peter van Gogh, Pieter Wiersma, Friso Broeksma, Mr. and Mrs. Nellens, W. Meulenkamp, G. Tomlow, The Landmark Trust, Bruno Weber, Family Brown, Tatin, Grandma Prisbrey, Mrs. Isidore, Jacques Verroust, Clovis Prevost, Ed van der Elsken, Mary Unthank, Greg Blasdel, Jan Wampler, Family Vasseur, Descharnes, Karin-Koehn, Mrs. Marian Grossman, Mr. Garcet, Fred Burns, Ad Peterson, Maarten Kloos, Prof. George R. Collins, and Nora Beeson.

One of Pieter Wiersma's sand sculptures.